T0339519

Cambridge Elements ≡

Elements in the Philosophy of Physics
edited by
James Owen Weatherall
University of California, Irvine

EMERGENCE AND REDUCTION IN PHYSICS

Patricia Palacios
University of Salzburg

CAMBRIDGE
UNIVERSITY PRESS

University Printing House, Cambridge CB2 8BS, United Kingdom

One Liberty Plaza, 20th Floor, New York, NY 10006, USA

477 Williamstown Road, Port Melbourne, VIC 3207, Australia

314–321, 3rd Floor, Plot 3, Splendor Forum, Jasola District Centre, New Delhi – 110025, India

103 Penang Road, #05–06/07, Visioncrest Commercial, Singapore 238467

Cambridge University Press is part of the University of Cambridge.

It furthers the University's mission by disseminating knowledge in the pursuit of education, learning, and research at the highest international levels of excellence.

www.cambridge.org
Information on this title: www.cambridge.org/9781108814065
DOI: 10.1017/9781108901017

First published 2022 ·

A catalogue record for this publication is available from the British Library.

ISBN 978-1-108-81406-5 Paperback
ISSN 2632-413X (online)
ISSN 2632-4121 (print)

Emergence and Reduction in Physics

Elements in the Philosophy of Physics

DOI: 10.1017/9781108901017
First published online: September 2022

Patricia Palacios
University of Salzburg

Author for correspondence: Patricia Palacios, patricia.palacios@plus.ac.at

Abstract: This Element offers an overview of some of the most important debates in philosophy and physics around the topics of emergence and reduction and proposes a compatibilist view of emergence and reduction. In particular, it suggests that specific notions of emergence, which the author calls "few-many emergence" and "coarse-grained emergence," are compatible with "intertheoretic reduction." Some further issues that will be addressed concern the comparison between parts-whole emergence and few-many emergence, the emergence of effective (-field) theories, the use of infinite limits, the notion of intertheoretic reduction, and the explanation of universal and cooperative behavior. Although the focus will be principally on classical phase transitions and other examples from condensed matter physics, the main aim is to draw some general conclusions on the topics of emergence and reduction that can help us understand a variety of case studies ranging from high-energy physics to astrophysics.

Keywords: emergence, reduction, intertheoretic reduction, renormalization group methods, critical phenomena

ISBNs: 9781108814065 (PB), 9781108901017 (OC)
ISSNs: 2632-413X (online), 2632-4121 (print)

Contents

1 Introduction

The topic of emergence and reduction is nowadays one of the liveliest areas of research in both physics and philosophy. The reason for this is related to recent developments in a number of successful research programs within condensed matter physics, statistical mechanics, and quantum field theory, among others. Such developments have encouraged philosophers and physicists to rethink the relationship between cooperative systems and their parts as well as the relationship between different theories.

Especially in the past twenty years, physicists and philosophers have been involved in fervent debates on different issues associated with the topic of emergence and reduction by focusing on concrete case studies. Indeed, traditional philosophical discussions on intertheoretic reduction, synchronic and diachronic emergence, supervenience, and microphysicalism have now been reframed on the basis of particular case studies within specific fields of physics ranging from quantum gravity to condensed matter physics. The biggest advantage of this recent specialization is that the philosophical debate is nowadays scientifically informed and more relevant to the scientific practice. The biggest disadvantage, however, is that it is becoming more and more difficult to keep track of the relevant literature and to achieve a comprehensive understanding of recent developments on this topic.

The previous remarks raise the question of how we shall approach such a tantalizing topic in an introductory Element. There are two main strategies that one could follow: top-down or bottom-up. Top-down would mean to start by defining our terms and then give examples of each of them from different areas of physics. Bottom-up would mean to start by explaining some putative examples of emergence and reduction and then construct different concepts of emergence and reduction that fit with them. Although many authors prefer to follow the top-down strategy, I will adopt the bottom-up approach, especially because, as I will argue here, there is no uncontroversial characterization of emergence that can fit well with all putative cases of emergent behavior.

Our main example, although by no means the only one, will be the case of classical phase transitions, which are sudden changes in the phenomenological properties of a system that we observe, for instance, when liquid water turns into vapor. There are plenty of reasons why phase transitions have been chosen as the principal example in our exploration of this topic. First of all, phase transitions are a prime example of Philip Anderson's celebrated paper "More is different," which reinitiated the discussion on emergence in physics in 1972.[1]

---

[1] The discussion on emergence in science can be traced back to the "British Emergentism," a movement that began in the middle of the nineteenth century and lasted until the first quarter of

Second, classical phase transitions have been at the center of different debates on emergence and reduction in physics, including discussions on intertheoretic reduction, emergence in effective field theories (EFTs), multiple realizability, and singular limits. Third, these phenomena have characteristic properties that can help us understand more complicated case studies in other areas of physics and outside of physics. In fact, they are paradigm examples of cooperative behavior, self-organization, power-law behavior, scale invariance, spontaneous symmetry breaking (SSB), and universality. Finally, classical phase transitions have the advantage of being simple or at least simpler than other case studies often discussed in these debates. Yet, classical phase transitions allow us to draw general conclusions on the topic of emergence and reduction that can help us improve our understanding of other putative cases of emergence in physics and can even help us revise previous notions of emergence and reduction in physics.

Although the strategy that I follow in this Element is bottom-up, which means I will draw some general conclusions on the concepts of emergence and reduction by focusing on specific case studies, it is important to start by explaining some preliminary concepts. These concepts will function as directions that will help us develop specific notions of emergence throughout this Element. In the next section, I will explain these concepts and in Section 1.2, I will describe in greater detail the plan and the aims of this Element.

1.1 Preliminary Concepts: The Emergence Landscape

Many philosophers agree that there is no single definition of emergence that can account for all putative cases of emergent behavior in physics. For instance, in a recent book on emergence, Humphreys (2016) says "there does not exist, and I believe there will not exist in the near future, a single, overarching theoretical framework for [emergence]" (p. xvii). However, most philosophers seem to agree that there are some basic notions that can help us frame the discussion around emergence and reduction. For instance, there seems to be a consensus in the literature that emergence is a relation between two *relata*, that is, the *emergent* and the *basis*, which satisfies at least two theses: one establishing a certain *dependence* of the emergent upon the basis and the other establishing a certain *independence* of the former upon the latter (Guay and Sartenaer, 2016; Humphreys, 2016; O'Connor and Wong, 2015). The interpretation of

---

the twentieth century. In the early 1930s, the interest in emergence progressively declined due, in part, to advances in quantum chemistry and molecular biology such as the discovery of DNA (Humphreys, 2016).

these relata as well as the interpretation of the dependence/independence theses depends on the type of emergence under investigation.

In order to construct specific concepts of emergence and therefore to give a particular interpretation to the previous terms, it is useful to take into account historical distinctions in the philosophical literature on emergence. Guay and Sartenaer (2016) emphasize the following three distinctions that I will take as a basis to construct more specific notions of emergence in the next sections:

(i) **Ontological versus epistemological:** *Epistemological emergence* is associated with limitations in our knowledge of the natural world rather than with the world itself. In general, a behavior (property or pattern) is said to be epistemologically emergent, for instance, if it cannot be explained, predicted, or derived from the corresponding basis or if it is described in terms that do not appear in the basis, which means that the terms are *novel* with respect to the basis. On the other hand, *ontological emergence* requires the emergent to be ontologically distinct from its basis. Although lack of explanation, prediction, or derivation can be taken as evidence for ontological emergence, one needs further arguments to conclude that the emergence is not merely epistemological, but also ontological. Indeed, ontological emergence is usually presented in terms of new causal powers, or new fundamental laws (Guay and Sartenaer, 2016; O'Connor and Wong, 2015).

(ii) **Weak versus strong:** *Weak emergence* affirms the autonomy of the emergent (e.g. high-level phenomena or high-level laws) with respect to the corresponding basis, while still affirming *microphysicalism*, namely the thesis that all natural phenomena are wholly constituted from fundamental microphysical entities and metaphysically determined by the fundamental laws of physics, whether particle physics, quantum field theory, quantum gravity, or some other unknown theory.[2] On the other hand, *strong emergence* maintains that at least some emergents (e.g. high-level phenomena or high-level laws) exhibit a weaker dependence or stronger autonomy than weak emergence allows (O'Connor and Wong, 2015). This often implies a rejection of the thesis of microphysicalism and a rejection of supervenience, which roughly says that there cannot be a difference at the level of the emergent without a difference at the level of the basis (Section 4.3). Sometimes weak/strong emergence is defined in terms of lack of derivability in practice/in principle (e.g. Chalmers, 2006; Ellis, 2020;

---

[2] Microphysicalism is consistent with the "physical causal closure." This thesis says that every lower-level physical effect has a purely lower-level physical cause (O'Connor and Wong, 2015).

Guay and Sartenaer, 2016). However, I will argue in Sections 3.3 and 4.4. that this definition is not ideal, since it can lead to confusion, especially when we focus on the case of phase transitions and EFTs.

(iii) **Diachronic versus synchronic:** *Diachronic emergence* emphasizes the emergence of novel behavior, novel properties, or novel patterns "across time." This is sometimes formulated as a dynamical evolution of the system from pre- to post-complexity stages (Guay and Sartenaer, 2016). In contrast, *synchronic emergence* emphasizes the coexistence of novel "higher level" behavior, properties, or laws with respect to behavior, properties, or laws existing at some "lower level" (Humphreys, 2008).

These distinctions will help us construct more specific notions of emergence in the following sections. In particular, they will help us understand (i) *parts-whole emergence* (Section 3.1), which means that the properties (or behavior) of the whole system are novel with respect to the properties (or behavior) of its component parts "taken in isolation," (ii) *few-many emergence* (Sections 3.1 and 3.4), which means that the properties (or behavior) of systems with very many components are novel with respect to the properties (or behavior) of systems with fewer components, and (iii) *coarse-grained emergence* (Section 4.3), which implies that a coarse-grained description of a given system is autonomous and has terms that are novel with respect to a fine-grained description.

Throughout this Element, we will also distinguish between different notions of reduction. In particular, in Section 3, we will distinguish between *few-many reduction* (as opposed to few-many emergence) and *parts-whole reduction* (as opposed to parts-whole emergence). In Section 5, we will focus instead on *intertheoretic reduction*, which describes a relationship between different theories.

1.2 Prospectus

This Element has three main aims. The first is to introduce the reader to some of the most important discussions on the topic of emergence and reduction in physics by focusing mainly on the case of classical phase transitions and other similar case studies. The second goal is to evaluate to what extent phase transitions, which have been at the center of the most interesting controversies on this topic, are successful instances of emergence and reduction. In particular, I will argue that critical phase transitions instantiate two different notions of emergence that I call "few-many" and "coarse-grained" emergence. At the same time, I will contend that they are successful cases of intertheoretic reduction. The third aim is to draw some general lessons on the topic of emergence and reduction on the basis of the chosen case studies. The first lesson is that emergence is compatible with intertheoretic reduction, a thesis that has been systematically defended by Butterfield (2011a; 2011b) and is slowly reaching a consensus within the philosophical literature. So instead of defining emergence in terms of "lack of derivability" or "lack of reduction," I will emphasize the importance of novelty and autonomy in the different characterizations of emergence. The second lesson is that intertheoretic reduction should be rather understood as a family of different models that can be combined in order to achieve certain epistemological and ontological goals. The third lesson concerns the notion of "singular limits." Contra some authors (e.g. Batterman, 2001, 2005; Rueger, 2000, 2004), I will argue that the use of singular limits is neither sufficient nor necessary for emergence and that they can be explained away in favor of intertheoretic reduction, at least in the cases under investigation.

The plan of this Element is as follows: In Section 2, I will introduce the reader to the most basic aspects of the physics of phase transitions, which will be considered a prime example of emergent behavior. The reader who is already familiar with the physics of phase transitions should feel free to skip this section. In Section 3, I will discuss the notions of "few-many emergence" and "few-many reduction" by focusing on examples from condensed matter physics and I will contrast these notions with the notion of "parts-whole emergence." I will contend that whereas first-order phase transitions are a case of few-many reduction, continuous phase transitions are a case of few-many emergence. In Section 4, I will discuss the use of renormalization group (RG) methods in condensed matter physics and I will argue that they should be associated with a different notion of emergence, which I call "coarse-grained emergence." I will argue that this notion can also be used to characterize a set of EFTs. In Section 5, I will focus on the notion of intertheoretic reduction and will address discussions on singular limits. I will suggest that we should understand intertheoretic reduction as a family of models that help us achieve certain goals. I will finally conclude that intertheoretic reduction so understood is compatible with the notions of emergence developed in the previous sections.

2 Phase Transitions: A Paradigm Case

Phase transitions are those drastic changes in the phenomenological properties of a system that we observe, for instance, when liquid water transforms into vapor. In thermodynamics, phase transitions are described in terms of discontinuities or singularities (i.e. nonanalyticities) in functions that represent physical quantities, such as the entropy S, the volume V, and the specific heat

C. For example, when water boils and changes to vapor, the volume V appears to change discontinuously. From a thermodynamic point of view, the reason behind the occurrence of such a phase transition is the competition between the (internal) energy E and the entropy S of the system, which together determine its free energy $F = E - TS$. While the first term E favors order, the second S privileges disorder, and depending on the value of the external parameters such as temperature T, one of the two terms dominates. Generally, phase transitions can be classified into two main groups: first-order phase transitions and continuous transitions. The distinction between these two kinds of phase transitions plays an important role in the discussion on emergence and reduction in physics. Therefore, it is convenient to spend some time in describing these two kinds of transitions in greater detail, which is the task of the present section.

2.1 First-Order Phase Transitions

In thermodynamics, first-order phase transitions are defined as discontinuities (or "jumps") in the first-order derivatives of the free energy F. For instance, the transition from ice to water involves a jump in the entropy $\Delta S > 0$, which is a first derivative of the free energy $S = -(\partial F/\partial T)_V$. Another example of first-order phase transition is in magnetic materials. If the temperature T is low (lower than the so-called *critical temperature* T_c), the sign of the magnetization m jumps from negative values to positive values as the external magnetic field h is scanned from the negative direction to the positive direction, as illustrated in Figure 1. Microscopically this can be qualitatively understood as follows. For negative values of h, the spins in the magnetic material align with that negative direction and they "suddenly" change direction as the external field becomes positive.

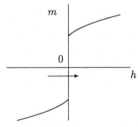

Figure 1 First-order phase transition in magnetic materials. The sign of the magnetization m jumps from minus to plus when the external field is scanned from the positive direction to the negative direction

From the statistical mechanical point of view, the thermodynamic treatment of phase transitions arises from the free energy, which is determined by the partition function Z:

$$Z = e^{-F/k_B T} = \mathrm{Tr}\, e^{-H/k_B T}, \tag{2.1}$$

where k_B is Boltzmann's constant, and Tr (trace) represents the sum over all the degrees of freedom that enter the Hamiltonian H of the system. The free energy can be then written as:

$$F[K_n] = -k_B T \log Z, \tag{2.2}$$

where $[K_n]$ is the set of coupling constants, which are the relevant external parameters such as field exchange and temperature.

Since the Hamiltonian is usually a nonsingular function of the degrees of freedom, the partition function Z is nothing more than a sum of terms, each of which represents an exponential of an analytic function. Such a quantity does not display the discontinuities that describe first-order phase transitions in thermodynamics as long as we consider finite systems. However, discontinuities or nonanalyticities of the free energy can be recovered in the *thermodynamic limit*, in which the volume V of the system as well as the number of degrees of freedom (e.g. spins in magnetic materials), N, go to infinity in such a way that the ratio remains constant, that is, $N/V \to const$. The use of the thermodynamic limit leads to interesting discussions around the topic of emergence and idealizations in physics. This is because one assumes that phase transitions occur in real systems like a teapot, which contain a finite number of particles. It is therefore puzzling that in order to account for this phenomenological behavior, one needs to invoke idealizations involving infinite number of particles. We will address discussions around this issue in Sections 3 and 5.

In statistical mechanical treatments of phase transitions, the use of *idealized models* is very common, which help in computing the partition function of real systems or at least reducing it to quadrature (i.e. a finite number of integrals rather than an infinite number of them). There are plenty of idealized models that serve to describe a class of real phase transitions such as the Ising model, the Heisenberg model, the Potts model, the Baxter model, and so on. The most popular model is the Ising model, which was originally developed to describe ferromagnetism.[3] The nearest neighbor Hamiltonian of the Ising model is defined as follows:

$$H = -J \sum_{\langle ij \rangle}^{N} S_i S_j - h \sum_i S_i, \tag{2.3}$$

---

[3] The Ising model has been widely discussed in the philosophy of science literature. For some (e.g. Weisberg, 2007) it consists of a "minimalistic model," which is a model that only maintains the factors that make the difference for the occurrence of the phenomenon. For others (Batterman and Rice, 2014) it consists of a "minimal model" that leaves out irrelevant details.

where S_i is the Ising spin ($S_i = \pm 1$) at site (lattice site) i, and $\langle ij \rangle$ represents an interacting spin pair. The coefficient J is the interaction constant (coupling constant) and h represents the external magnetic field expressed in units of energy in magnetic materials. In two dimensions, the Ising model can be thought of as an array of spins on a square lattice (Figure 2).

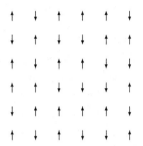

Figure 2 The two-dimensional Ising model with square lattice

The thermodynamic properties of the Ising model can be obtained by differentiation. If we assume that there is a uniform external magnetic field h, one can express the magnetization or magnetic moment per site M as follows:

$$M = \frac{1}{N}\frac{\partial F}{\partial h}. \tag{2.4}$$

In one dimension, the model does not display any phase transition, but in dimensions $d \geq 2$, the model can display a phase transition in the thermodynamic limit.

The Ising model has been used extensively as a model of magnetism in which J denotes the exchange interaction; however, the model can also be used to describe phase transitions in different types of systems, including the transition from liquid water to vapor.

2.2 Critical Phenomena

In contrast to first-order phase transitions, *continuous phase transitions* are not defined in terms of discontinuities in the first derivatives of the free energy but rather in terms of divergences in the response functions (e.g. susceptibility for a magnet, compressibility for a fluid). These kinds of transitions are often synonymous with *critical phenomena*, which are defined as anomalous phenomena that appear around the *critical point*, which is when two or more phases become indistinguishable.

Continuous phase transitions abound in physics. Examples of this kind of transition are the critical liquid-gas transition (represented in Figure 3), the paramagnetic–ferromagnetic transition in magnetic materials (represented in

Figure 4), the superfluid transition in liquid helium 4, and the Kosterlitz–Thouless transition.

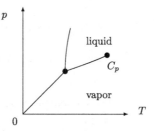

Figure 3 Phase diagram for water, where p is pressure, T is temperature, and C_p is the critical point. The boundaries represent first-order phase transitions. The gas–liquid phase boundary ends at C_p. Beyond the critical point, associated with a critical temperature T_c, the system can go from one phase to another without encountering a first-order phase transition

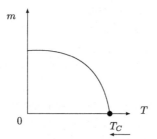

Figure 4 Continuous phase transition in magnetic materials. Below the critical temperature, the system is in a *ferromagnetic phase* and there is a net magnetization M

The main properties of critical phenomena can be illustrated by the example of the ferromagnetic–paramagnetic transition in magnetic materials (Figure 4). At high temperatures (much higher than the critical temperature T_c), the system is in a *paramagnetic phase* without net magnetization M. If we decrease the temperature to just above the critical temperature T_c, the magnetization increases very rapidly for a small but finite external field h. At the critical temperature, the magnetization grows even more rapidly as a function of the external field $\chi \propto h^{1/\delta}(1/\delta < 1)$, and the magnetic susceptibility χ, defined as the change of magnetization with respect to the external field, diverges as $h \to 0$.

Below the critical temperature, the system is in a *ferromagnetic phase* and there is a net magnetization M. The onset of the transition from paramagnetism to ferromagnetism is a continuous phase transition, in which the magnetization rises continuously from zero as the temperature is reduced below T_c (Figure 4).

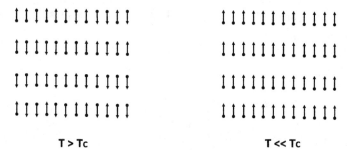

Figure 5 Phase transition from paramagnetic (left) to ferromagnetic phase (right), when the temperature T is reduced to values that are much lower than the critical temperature $T \ll T_c$

Microscopically, one can describe the situation as follows. At high temperatures, the spins are randomly distributed and do not spontaneously align, but as T gets closer to the critical temperature T_c, they tend to have a similar direction within fairly large regions, thus increasing the value of the magnetization very rapidly. Below the critical temperature, the spins tend to align along a particular direction in space, so there will be a net magnetization M, even if the external magnetic field is zero (Figure 5). This process is sometimes referred to as *self-organization*, since there is no influence of an external field.

The transition from a paramagnetic phase to a ferromagnetic phase is dominated by fluctuations in the degree of alignment of spins, which are reflected by singularities in some physical quantities. The same behavior is observed around the liquid–vapor critical point illustrated in Figure 3. Close to the critical point, large clusters of high density appear in the vapor, which can be described as fluctuations in the density. Crucially, the length scale of such fluctuations in critical phenomena ranges from microscopic to quasi-macroscopic near the critical point. In fact, there are fluctuations of length scales close to the wavelength of visible light, which appear as white cloud-like regions in the transparent liquid/vapor. This phenomenon is known as *critical opalescence*.

Another important property of critical phenomena is that near the critical point, the behavior of the physical quantities is governed by power laws associated with critical exponents. In simple magnetic materials, these critical exponents are defined as follows:

$$\chi \propto |t|^{-\gamma} \ (T > T_c),$$
$$C \propto |t|^{-\alpha} \ (T > T_c), \tag{2.5}$$
$$m \propto |t|^{\beta} \ (T < T_c),$$

where χ is the magnetic susceptibility, C is the specific heat, M is the magnetization and t is the reduced temperature defined as $t = (T - T_c)/T_c$.

Finally, as stated at the beginning of this section, continuous phase transitions are characterized by the divergence of some physical quantities at the transition or critical point. The critical exponents α and γ are typically (although not always) positive, so that the power laws that have negative exponents (and the corresponding quantities like specific heat and susceptibility) diverge as $T \rightarrow T_c$. The divergence of the magnetic susceptibility χ implies the divergence of the *correlation length* ξ, a quantity that measures the distance over which the spins or groups of spins are correlated, which also obeys power-law behavior: $\xi \propto |t|^{-\nu}$. The divergence of the correlation length is perhaps the most important feature of continuous phase transitions because it involves the loss of a characteristic length scale at the transition point and thus provides a basis for *universality*, which is the most remarkable feature of critical phase transitions. Universality is the striking similarity in the behavior near the critical point among different systems. What makes this similarity in the behavior of different systems more intriguing is that it is not only qualitative but also quantitative. In fact, a class of different systems as diverse as fluids and ferromagnets has been shown to share the same values of critical exponents within the accuracy of the experiments. For instance, the critical exponent β for the ferromagnetic critical point has the same value as the one that describes the behavior of the density at the liquid–gas critical phase transition $|\rho_+ - \rho_-| \propto |t|^\beta$ (details in Goldenfeld, 1992, pp. 5–19; Nishimori and Ortiz, 2010, pp. 16–26). The systems that behave in the same way near the critical point are said to be members of the same *universality class*. For instance, the three-dimensional Ising model, the liquid–gas critical transition and the ferromagnetic–paramagnetic transition are all members of the same universality class.

Critical phenomena and their characteristic features have given rise to the most interesting discussions around emergence and reduction in physics and most of this Element will be devoted to the analysis of this phenomenon with the goal of drawing some general conclusions around emergence and reduction. But before we start with the philosophical discussion, it is convenient to describe some of the properties of critical phenomena in more detail.

2.3 Scale Invariance and Universality

As mentioned in the last section, one of the most important properties of critical phenomena is that, exactly at the critical point, fluctuations of all length scales appear simultaneously, causing nonanalytical behavior of some physical quantities. This means that there is an absence of typical length scale. In fact,

Figure 6 A Koch curve as an example of scale invariance

fluctuations exist on all scales and all scales are equally important. Moreover, these fluctuations are scale invariant, in the sense that they are statistically self-similar up to the scale ξ, which represents the correlation length.

In order to understand what underlies the idea of scale invariance, it is useful to start by examining a simple example. Let us consider a 1 cm × 1 cm square. This square can be transformed without losing its form into a 1 in × 1 in square by multiplying the length of each side by 2.54. In order to transform the area we multiply by $(2.54)^2$. More generally, any two square areas can be connected by the transformation:

$$A'(\lambda L) = \lambda^2 A(L), \tag{2.6}$$

where L is the length scale of the square (the length of one side) and λ is the *scaling transformation*.

The same self-similar or scale-invariant behavior arises in fractals, which are geometrical models generated recursively. An example of fractals is the Koch curve illustrated in Figure 6, which is generated by trisecting each side of the original figure, erecting a small equilateral triangle on the central section, and repeating this process indefinitely (details in McComb, 2004, pp. 42–44).

Scale invariance constitutes the key ingredient to understand critical phenomena and, moreover, provides a basis for universality, the remarkable fact that different systems have the same values of critical exponents near a phase transition.[4] The first attempt to explain universality by appealing to scale invariance was suggested by L. P. Kadanoff (1996). Based on experimental evidence, he assumed that near the critical point, the system should "look the

---

[4] See Franklin (2019) for a detailed analysis of the relationship between scale invariance and universality.

same on all length scales," which implies that the form of the Hamiltonian must remain invariant under the application of a series of coarse-graining transformations that progressively wash out inessential short-range details. This coarse-graining procedure was meant to demonstrate that the macroscopic behavior exhibited by critical phenomena does not depend on short-range details that characterize specific models, but rather on a subset of essential features that are common within the members of the universality class.

Although Kadanoff's argument proved to be, strictly speaking, incorrect, indeed the Hamiltonian does not remain invariant under coarse-graining transformations, it provided the basic physical insight on which Wilson's RG methods were built and constituted the first step toward an explanation of universality. In Section 4, I will explain how Wilson's RG methods completed Kadanoff's argument, by offering an explanation of universality and the possibility of estimating the critical exponents.

2.4 Spontaneous Symmetry Breaking

Maybe one of the most important reasons why phase transitions are at the core of recent discussions on emergence and reduction in physics is that for a large class of phase transitions, the system undergoes a *symmetry change* or *SSB*. Roughly, SSB means that the symmetries of the original system are broken or lost. As an example, let us consider again the paramagnetic–ferromagnetic transition illustrated in Figure 5. At a high temperature, the spins are disordered (left panel in Figure 5) and the relevant quantities of the system, such as the net magnetization, are invariant under "up-down" symmetry $\{S_i\} \rightarrow \{-S_i\}$, that is, they remain the same if we flip all the spins, so as to change their direction:

$$M = \frac{1}{N} \sum_i \langle S_i \rangle = \frac{1}{N} \sum_i \langle -S_i \rangle = 0. \tag{2.7}$$

However, if the temperature is below the critical temperature T_c (right panel in Figure 5), this symmetry will be *spontaneously broken* and the transformation $\{S_i\} \rightarrow \{-S_i\}$ will no longer maintain the value of the net magnetization, changing the value of the magnetization from negative values to positive values (or the other way around).[5] The word "spontaneous" here means that this process occurs in the absence of an external magnetic field, that is, in the limit $h \rightarrow 0$.

It is important to point out that, strictly speaking, SSB in magnetic materials (and correspondingly, spontaneous magnetization), in which $h = 0$, cannot

---

[5] In fact, only one of the two equilibria states M_+ or M_- will be realized, which does not remain invariant under the overall change of the signs of spins.

occur in finite systems. This is a consequence of the up-down symmetry of the Hamiltonian that determines the free energy and therefore the values of the magnetization (details in Goldenfeld, 1992, pp. 50–51).[6] However, spontaneous magnetization can arise if we take the thermodynamic limit followed by the limit $h \to 0$:[7]

$$M = \lim_{h \to 0} \lim_{N \to \infty} \frac{1}{N} \frac{\partial F}{\partial h} \neq 0. \tag{2.8}$$

SSB is a crucial feature of modern physics and has been at the center of important debates on the topic of emergence and reduction (Fraser, 2016; Landsman, 2013; Morrison, 2012). In fact, the phenomenon of SSB occupies a central role in Anderson's celebrated "More Is Different," which, as stated earlier, resuscitated the discussion on emergence in physics. In that paper, SSB can be interpreted as a *mechanism* for emergent behavior (Mainwood, 2006). Some authors, most notably Morrison (2012), have even suggested that SSB is *necessary* for the occurrence of emergent behavior. She justifies this view by arguing that SSB gives a dynamical explanation of emergent phenomena, which does not depend on the microscopic details of model systems.

Although Morrison's contention seems to fit well with the case of superconductivity (a phase transition in magnetic materials toward a state with flux quantization and zero resistivity), which she considers a paradigmatic example of emergent behavior, it is questionable whether this can be extended to all types of phase transitions, and more generally to all cases of emergent behavior. Bain (2013a), for instance, discusses many candidates for emergent behavior, which do not involve any symmetry breaking, such as the transition from a less-ordered conductor state to a more-ordered quantum Hall liquid state, which will be discussed in Section 4.4 of this Element.

2.5 Concluding Remarks

In this section, we have introduced the most important aspects of the physics of phase transitions, distinguishing between first-order and continuous phase transitions and emphasizing notable properties of the latter such as scale invariance, universality, and symmetry-breaking. This will help us address many different issues on the topic of emergence and reduction in the following sections.

---

[6] There is an important discussion on the apparent need for the thermodynamic limit in the explanation of SSB (see Fraser, 2016; Landsman, 2013; Wallace, 2018). Although this discussion will not be reviewed here, we will address a similar discussion concerning the apparent need for the thermodynamic limit in the explanation of phase transitions (Sections 3.3, 5.3, 5.4).

[7] Note that these limits do not commute. If we take $N \to \infty$ after $h \to 0$, there will be no net magnetization (Goldenfeld, 1992, p. 51).

Although the analysis will be mainly focused on the phenomena of phase transitions and other similar examples, the goal is to draw some general morals on the topic of emergence and reduction, which should serve to improve our understanding on this topic and help us understand other putative cases of reduction and emergence in physics.

3 Few-Many Reduction versus Few-Many Emergence

Phase transitions and their characteristic properties have been at the center of recent debates around reduction and emergence in physics. For some, phase transitions are instances of successful reductions, while for others they constitute the hallmark of emergence. Not so many years ago, Butterfield (2011a, 2011b, 2014) and Norton (2014) suggested that phase transitions combine both emergence and reduction. This alleged compatibility relies on a careful distinction between two notions that Norton (2014) dubbed as "few-many emergence" (as opposed to "few-many reduction") and "intertheoretic reduction." In this section, I will focus on the former, whereas the latter will be addressed in Section 5. In Section 4, I will discuss a different notion of emergence that I call "coarse-grained emergence."

3.1 Parts-Whole Emergence and Few-Many Emergence

The notion of few-many reduction is implicit in Anderson's seminal paper "More Is Different" and describes the relationship between two different scales: the scale describing the behavior of a system with very many components and the scale describing the behavior of a few components. In successful cases of few-many reduction, it is possible to use a variety of approximation methods, such as mean-field approximations, perturbation expansions, and virial expansions to reconstruct the aggregate behavior of a system with many particles from the properties of small clusters of atoms. Correspondingly, a failure of few-many reduction, or what we call here "few-many emergence," means that one cannot extrapolate the behavior of a system with a large number of components by studying a small sample of it.

More precisely, few-many emergence can be defined as follows:

> **Few-many emergence:** A system exhibits few-many emergence when there is a robust behavior (pattern or property) at the scale of many components that is epistemologically/ontologically novel with respect to the scale of few components.

Let us explain the terms of this definition:

(i) *The few/many distinction:* In "few-many" emergence, one distinguishes between the scale that describes the behavior of the very many particles in the system (sometimes this system is conceptually infinite) and the scale describing the behavior of just two or a few particles. How many particles count as "a few" depends on the case study. In general, scientists are interested in extrapolating the global behavior of many-particle systems by studying systems with no more than a dozen of atoms.[8] Few-many emergence should be rather interpreted as an *intra-level relation*, since in both cases, we focus on the same molecular statistical level of description (Norton, 2014).

(ii) *Epistemological novelty:* The global behavior of the system with many components is epistemologically novel with respect to the behavior of smaller systems, if the former can neither be *explained* nor *predicted* from the latter (Kim, 1999). Some authors (e.g. Broad, 1925 [2014], Goldstein, 1999) define epistemological novelty in terms of "lack of derivability in practice."

(iii) *Ontological novelty:* The behavior of a system with many particles is ontologically novel with respect to the behavior of systems with a smaller number of particles, if the former is ontologically distinct from the latter and is a feature of the world itself. Some authors (e.g. Batterman, 2001; Bedau, 2002; Broad, 1925 [2014]; Smart, 1981) also understand ontological emergence in terms of "lack of deducibility in principle." Although lack of derivability may suggest that there is ontological emergence, we will argue in Section 3.3 that this is not the best way of defining ontological novelty.

(iv) *Robustness:* The emergent behavior of the many-particle system is generally robust, in the sense that it does not depend on the behavior of a few components or a specific arrangement of components. In other words, there is insensitivity to variations of different arrangement of components.

(v) *Dependence:* The emergent behavior of the many-particle system "depends" on the behavior of systems with a fewer number of components in that the former is assumed to be *constituted* by the same kind of degrees of freedom than the latter.

The notion of few-many emergence can be made more precise by taking into account the distinction made in Section 1.1 between *weak* and *strong*

---

[8] For instance, Bayha and colleagues (2020) studied the behavior of systems exhibiting quantum phase transitions by focusing on the behavior of two, six, and twelve fermionic atoms in the ground state.

emergence. If systems with many particles (i) are ultimately constituted by the same kind of degrees of freedom than smaller system and (ii) obey the same fundamental laws that govern the behavior of smaller systems, then few-many emergence is weak rather than strong. This is because if conditions (i) and (ii) are fulfilled, microphysicalism (i.e. the thesis that all natural phenomena are wholly constituted from fundamental microphysical entities and metaphysically determined by the fundamental laws of physics) is secured. I will argue that the case studies analyzed in this section are cases of weak rather than strong emergence.

Although the notions of few-many emergence and, correspondingly, few-many reduction occupy a central role in the physics literature, especially in condensed matter physics, they have received surprisingly little attention in the philosophical literature. In fact, most of the philosophical discussion on emergence has focused on a similar but not equivalent notion of "parts-whole emergence," which is generally interpreted as an *inter-level relation* between the behavior of the whole system (macro-level) and the behavior of all its parts taken in isolation (micro-level) (Guay and Sartenaer, 2016).[9]

Let us examine the notion of parts-whole emergence in more detail. The concept of parts-whole emergence can be traced back to the British Emergentism, which was a movement that existed from the middle of the nineteenth century until the early decades of the twentieth century. Perhaps the most influential member of the British Emergentist movement was C. D. Broad, who was particularly concerned about the relationship between the properties exhibited by composite systems and the properties exhibited by their parts "taken in isolation." A prototypical example of parts-whole emergence in his book *The Mind and His Place in Nature* (1925 [2014]) was the relation between the properties of the chemical compound silver – chloride and the properties of both silver and chlorine taken in isolation.

In the book, Broad characterizes emergence in the following terms:

> [T]he characteristic properties of the whole R(A, B, C) [where A, B and C refers to the constituent components and R to their structural arrangement] cannot, even in theory, be deduced from the most complete knowledge of the properties of A, B, and C in isolation or in other wholes which are not of the form R(A, B, C)." (Broad, 1925 [2014], p. 61)

Following Broad's characterization of parts-whole emergence, one can define this type of emergence as follows:

---

[9] A notable exception to this are the papers by Butterfield (2011a, 2011b) and Norton (2014), which explicitly focus on the notion of few-many emergence.

> **Parts-whole emergence:** A system exhibits parts-whole emergence when
> the properties of the whole system are *novel* with respect to the properties of
> its parts taken *in isolation.*

Note that this notion of parts-whole emergence describes a synchronic relation, in which the whole and its parts are taken to coexist.[10] Note also that in
Broad's definition of parts-whole emergence, "novelty" is interpreted as the
impossibility of deducing, even in principle, the properties of the whole from
the most complete knowledge of the behavior of its component parts "taken in
isolation."[11]

Some philosophers (e.g. Mainwood, 2006; Norton, 2014) identify the concept of few-many emergence with parts-whole emergence, but I think it is
important to keep these two concepts separated. In fact, an important difference between these two types of emergence is that in parts-whole emergence,
one generally compares the holistic behavior of the system with the behavior of
(all) its components "taken in isolation." In contrast, in few-many emergence,
one is not interested in how the component parts behave in isolation, but rather
in comparing the behavior of the same *interacting system* (or analogous systems) at different scales of component number. More precisely, in the case
of few-many emergence, the scales of interest are specified by geometry and
we distinguish "micro" and "macro" scales according to their typical sizes. In
other words, what is important in few-many emergence is not the comparison
between the behavior of the whole system and the behavior of its constituent parts "taken in isolation," but rather the behavior of an interacting system
with many components and the behavior of a sample of this interacting system (or an analogous interacting system) with a fewer number of components.
Furthermore, in contrast to parts-whole emergence, in the case of few-many
emergence, the smaller system may not be considered to be "a part" of the bigger system. Indeed, many times the extrapolation of the systemic properties
of the larger system is done by simulations in small independent systems. For

---

[10] Guay and Sartenaer (2016) have recently suggested a perspective shift in the notion of parts-
whole emergence, by focusing not on the synchronic relation between the whole and the
parts, but rather on the diachronic relation between the behavior of the parts taken in isolation at a time t_1 and the collective behavior that arises from their interactions at a later time
t_2.

[11] Sometimes "novelty" is understood here in causal terms. In this view, there is novelty, more
precisely *ontological novelty*, if the whole has causal powers of its own, which are not reducible
to the causal powers of its parts (Gillett, 2016; Hendry, 2010; Kim, 1999; Mill, 1872). Although
the notion of causation can be important to understand certain notions of emergence, especially
in the philosophy of mind, I will define different notions of emergence without invoking causal
terms.

instance, in a recent paper published in *Nature*, Bayha and colleagues (2020) used quantum simulation with a fairly small number of cold atoms (no more than twelve) to infer the behavior of a quantum phase transition from a normal to a superfluid phase.

Another difference between parts-whole emergence and few-many emergence is that whereas the former is usually interpreted as a synchronic relation, in few-many emergence, the temporal perspective does not seem to play any important role. In fact, the comparison between bigger and smaller systems can be done synchronically by simultaneously tracking the behavior of the bigger and smaller system or asynchronically by studying the systems at entirely different times, as when simulations of smaller systems are employed. Note also that the notion of constitution used to describe parts-whole relationships does not always apply to cases of few-many emergence. Indeed, the system with many components may not be constituted by the system with a few number of components, especially if the latter is not directly a part of the former. There is, however, a weaker and indirect sense in which the system with many components can be said to be "constituted" by the system with a few components, namely that the system with many components is usually assumed to have the same kind of degrees of freedom than the system with a small number of components.

The extrapolation from few to many components plays an important role in condensed matter physics. This is why it is more natural for condensed matter physicists to interpret relations of reduction and emergence as a relation between the scales of few and many components rather than as a relationship between wholes and parts. Anderson (1972), for instance, was interested in investigating symmetry-breaking phenomena by comparing systems with different size such as ammonia molecule and sugar. Although he did not mention the word "emergence" in his "More Is Different," he implicitly defined emergence in the following terms:

> The behaviour of large and complex aggregates of elementary particles, it turns out, is not to be understood in terms of a simple extrapolation of the properties of a few particles. Instead, at each level of complexity, entirely new properties appear, and the understanding of the new behaviours requires research, which I think is as fundamental in its nature as any other. (Anderson, 1972, p. 393)

Since we are mostly interested in examples from condensed matter physics, in the remainder of this section, we will focus on the notion of few-many emergence instead of parts-whole emergence.

3.2 From Few to Many: When More Is the Same

A simple yet idealized example of successful few-many reduction concerns the amount of energy in an ideal gas. Suppose that the ideal gas is constituted by microscopic particles assumed to be spherical, hard, and elastic, and suppose that the system has an amount of energy E. If we assume that the gas has a very low density, we can easily derive the relationship between the total energy of the gas and the energy of its constituent molecules. In fact, if all particles have the same mass m, the total energy of the ideal gas will be nothing more than the sum of all the kinetic energies of the molecules:

$$E = \frac{1}{2}mv_1^2 + \frac{1}{2}mv_2^2 + \ldots + \frac{1}{2}mv_N^2 = \frac{1}{2}m\sum_{j=1}^{N} v_j^2, \tag{3.1}$$

where $1/2mv_j^2$ is the kinetic energy of an individual molecule.

If the average speed of a molecule is $\bar{v}$, then the average kinetic energy per molecule is just the energy of the gas E divided by the number of molecules N:

$$\frac{1}{2}m\bar{v}^2 = \frac{E}{N} \tag{3.2}$$

Importantly, in order to estimate the total energy, one does not need to solve Eq. (3.1). Instead, one can extrapolate the macroscopic properties of the system, including the total energy, on the basis of a small sample of it. In fact, an ideal gas of 1,000 particles will probably have the same energy per unit volume as the gas with 10^{23} particles. Thus, this is a case where "few-many reduction" succeeds.

Another more realistic example is the crystalline solid. A microscopic model of this material consists of N identical particles on a three-dimensional lattice. In a quantum mechanical description, each particle will be in a potential well and will exist on some discrete energy level of the potential well. In other words, the jth particle will have access to the set of energy levels $\{\epsilon_1, \epsilon_2, \ldots, \epsilon_j, \ldots\}$, where ϵ_j denotes the energy levels of individual particles (for more details, see McComb, 2004, pp. 11–13). As in the case of the ideal gas, we can write the instantaneous energy E_i of the N-particle system as the sum of the instantaneous energy of the individual particles:

$$E_i = \epsilon_{i_1} + \epsilon_{i_2} + \ldots + \epsilon_{i_N}, \tag{3.3}$$

where particle 1 has energy ϵ_{i_1}, particle 2 has energy ϵ_{i_2}, and so on.

Since the individual particles will make transitions from one energy level to another, the total system energy E_i will fluctuate, with each value of i

corresponding to a realization defined by the numbers $\{i_1, i_2, \ldots, i_N\}$. The probability P of having a particular total energy E_i is given by:

$$P(E_i) = \frac{e^{-E_i/kT}}{Z},$$ (3.4)

where k is a constant and Z is the partition function or "sum over states," which in this case can be written as:

$$Z = \sum_{i_1, i_2, \ldots, i_3} exp[-(\epsilon_{i_1} + \epsilon_{i_2} + \ldots + \epsilon_{i_N})/kT].$$ (3.5)

Since this expression factorizes, one can write the single particle partition function Z_1 as

$$Z_1 = \sum_j exp[-E_j/kT].$$ (3.6)

Finally, the N-particle function can be expressed in terms of the single particle function as:

$$Z = Z_1^N.$$ (3.7)

The important lesson here is that the independence of the individual particles allows one to derive the partition function in terms of the energy levels of the individual particles. Moreover, as in the case of the ideal gas, one can extrapolate the macroscopic properties of the system like the energy per unit volume on the basis of a small sample of the system. Therefore, once again "few-many reduction" succeeds.

In the following section, I will describe the main aspects of mean-field theories and I will argue that in the case of first-order phase transitions, "few-many reduction" succeeds. In Section 3.4, I will focus on the case of critical phenomena and explain why the failure of mean-field theories suggests that the behavior of critical phase transitions is emergent with respect to the properties of a few number of particles.

3.3 First-Order Phase Transitions: Is "More" Really that Different?

The traditional strategy in statistical mechanics to study macroscopic phenomena such as phase transitions is to calculate the free energy, F, which is determined by the partition function Z:[12]

---

[12] Note that this expression is equivalent to Eq. (2.1)

$$Z = e^{-F/k_B T} = \sum_{states} e^{-H/k_B T}. \tag{3.8}$$

In an ideal scenario, one would expect to perform a direct calculation of the partition function and to solve models exactly. Unfortunately, analytic calculations of the partition function have been performed only in particular models with dimension $d = 1$ and $d = 2$; for all other cases, one requires approximation techniques.[13] The most important approximation used in the context of phase transitions is the mean-field approximation.[14] The basic idea of the mean-field theory is to focus on a single spin and replace the neighboring spins by their averages. In the mean-field approximation for the Ising model, the number of degrees of freedom can be dramatically reduced from 2^N to 2, which allows for the extrapolation of some qualitative macroscopic properties of the system from the properties of a fairly small sample of the system. Later in this Element, we will see that this procedure is equivalent to neglecting the fluctuations from the average value of the spins variables.

In order to understand how mean-field theories can make qualitative predictions, for instance, of first-order phase transitions, it is convenient to begin by studying a single Ising spin Hamiltonian in a magnetic field. This can be written as:

$$-H/T = h\sigma, \tag{3.9}$$

where σ represents a component of the spin in the direction of the magnetic field and h is the dimensionless magnetic field. Here k_B, the Boltzmann constant, is taken to be 1 for simplicity. The spin variable takes on two values ± 1, so that the probability of finding the spins with the two different values is:

$$\rho(+1) = e^h/Z \text{ and } \rho(-1) = e^{-h}/Z, \tag{3.10}$$

where $Z = e^h + e^{-h} = 2 \cosh h$, so that the average value of the spin is:

$$<\sigma> = e^h/Z - e^{-h}/Z = \tanh h. \tag{3.11}$$

Since the system is very small, statistical mechanics predicts that the average magnetization $< \sigma >$ will increase smoothly from -1 to 0 and from 0 to 1, when the the magnetic field increases smoothly from negative values to positive values (details in Kadanoff, 2009). Curie (1895) and Weiss (1907) derived an analogous equation for a system constituted by many particles by means of a

---

[13] The first and most famous exact solution of the partition function is the Onsager solution for an Ising model of dimension $d = 2$.

[14] There are actually many ways to generate mean field theories, so "mean-field theory" is a term that denotes a family of mean-field theories.

simplified mean-field theory of ferromagnetism. In this theory, they focused on one spin variable, σ_r, which "sees" a Hamiltonian defined by:

$$-H_r/T = \sigma_r[h(\mathbf{r}) + K \sum_{nn} < \sigma_s >] + constant, \qquad (3.12)$$

where $h(\mathbf{r})$ is the dimensionless magnetic field at point $\mathbf{r}$ and the sum includes all the spins with positions s, which are the nearest neighbors (nn) of $\mathbf{r}$. K are the coupling constants to the spins in the immediate neighborhood. This can be interpreted as if spin σ_r would "feel" a force coming from the applied field and the coupling constants of the immediate neighborhood. It is important to note that these effects, namely the effect of the applied field and the effect of the immediate neighborhood, are qualitatively different. Indeed, whereas the former is time-independent, the latter is not and fluctuates over time. However, in the mean-field theory, these two effects are simply added and the fluctuating values are replaced by their averages. Under this assumption, one can infer that the spin σ_r will obey the following equation:

$$< \sigma_r >= \tanh h^{eff}(\mathbf{r}). \qquad (3.13)$$

where h^{eff} is the "effective" or "mean" field.

If we assume that the system is big enough, so that boundary effects can be neglected, in other words, if we assume that there is space translation symmetry, Eq. (3.13) can be written more generally as:

$$< \sigma >= \tanh h^{eff}. \qquad (3.14)$$

Note that this equation has the same form as Eq. (3.11). If the temperature is very low, mean field theory correctly predicts that the magnetization falls into one of the two possible extreme values $< \sigma >= 1$ or $< \sigma >= -1$.

Note that what the mean-field approach does here is to extrapolate the mean or effective field for a many-particle system from a simple equation (Eq. 3.11), which is also appropriate for describing a single-particle system. The main difference between the single-particle case and the many-particle case is that in the latter, a first-order phase transition can occur even in the absence of an external magnetic field. Indeed, for a many-particle system at low temperatures, a positive value of the coupling K (Eq. 3.12) means that the two neighboring spins tend to line up with each other, which also help align the spin σ_r we are focusing on. For dimensions $d > 1$, this lining up will spread through the system by multiple chains of neighbor alignments, resulting in a global alignment in the system. Since we can extrapolate this qualitative behavior of the many-particle system by studying a small chunk of the big system and even by focusing on the behavior of a single particle in presence of an external field, this is a successful case of "few-many reduction."

It is worth mentioning, though, that some philosophers and physicists, most notably Batterman (2001) and Berry (2002), have argued against the previous conclusion, by pointing out that first-order phase transitions are only rigorously defined in the thermodynamic limit $V, N \rightarrow \infty$ (see Section 2.1). This means, according to them, that the behavior of the infinite system is qualitatively different from the behavior of a few particles, and furthermore, qualitatively different from the behavior of any finite system.

The idea that a phase transition can only be rigorously defined in the thermodynamic limit, at least in traditional approaches, is widely accepted in the physics community (e.g. Goldenfeld, 1992; Kadanoff, 2009, 2010) and is a consequence of defining first-order phase transitions in terms of discontinuities in the first derivatives of the free energy. As explained in Section 2.1, in statistical mechanics, the partition function Z, and therefore the free energy F is a sum of the exponentials of $-H/k_B T$ over all possible configurations. Such a sum of a finite number of exponentials is necessarily a positive quantity and will never display a discontinuity. Taking the thermodynamic limit allows one to derive the discontinuities in the free energy and thus allows for a rigorous definition of phase transitions. However, the use of the thermodynamic limit in the context of phase transitions does not imply that the behavior of the infinite system is real and qualitatively different from the behavior of finite systems. In fact, some philosophers and physicists have argued (e.g. Butterfield, 2011b; Fisher and Berker, 1982; Lavis et al., 2021; Menon and Callender, 2011; Palacios and Valente, 2021; Schmelzer et al., 2013) that the behavior that characterizes such a first-order phase transition can be qualitatively understood in finite systems and even quantitatively predicted up to a certain degree of approximation. We will come back to this discussion in Section 5.3, but for now let us recall the explanation of first-order phase transitions mentioned in this section. We saw that even in small systems, one can predict that the system will go smoothly from $<\sigma> = -1$ to $<\sigma> = 0$ to $<\sigma> = 1$, if the applied magnetic field increases from negative to positive values. As the number of particles N increases, one can predict that the change in the magnetization will occur more and more rapidly, that is, it will occur in a smaller and smaller interval around the applied field. This happens because a bigger system has more inertia than a smaller system (for details, see Butterfield, 2011b; Lavis et al., 2021).

Since there is no perfect experimental resolution, one needs to represent these changes in terms of discontinuities; however, there are many reasons to think that if one would have perfect resolution, one would be able to represent these changes as occurring over some range (for details, see Goldenfeld, 1992, p.

31; Lavis et al., 2021, pp. 46–50). Kadanoff (2009) expresses this idea in the following terms:

> For systems with fewer lattice sites the magnetization will vary slowly and continuously through zero as the field passes through zero. As the number of lattice sites gets larger the variation in the magnetization will get steeper, until at a very large number of sites the transition from positive values of $< \sigma >$ to negative ones will become so steep that the casual observer might say that it has occurred suddenly. The astute observer will look more closely, see that there is a very steep rise, and perhaps conclude that the discontinuous jump only occurs in the infinite system. (pp. 8–9)

The above discussion serves to illustrate a point made by Humphreys (2016, p. 9), namely that one should be very careful in distinguishing between the existence of emergence in models and the existence of emergence in the systems being modeled. In the case of first-order phase transitions, one may say that the *representation* of the phenomenon in terms of discontinuities in the derivatives of the free energy is not derivable, even in principle, from the properties of finite systems, at least from the perspective of conventional statistical mechanics. However, believing that this "failure of derivability in principle" implies that the real phenomena of phase transitions are ontologically novel and even strongly emergent with respect to the behavior of finite systems would be a mistake. As already mentioned, there are plenty of reasons to believe that the representation of phase transitions as discontinuities in the first derivatives of the free energy is only an approximation of the behavior of real systems, which actually display sharp but smooth transitions.[15]

It is also worth mentioning that in the past years, physicists have put forward alternative theories of phase transitions for "small" nonextensive systems, in which the entropy does not scale with the size of the system (e.g. Borrmann et al., 2000; Casetti et al., 2003; Gross, 2001). These alternative approaches may also be taken to support the conclusion that the definition of phase transitions as strict discontinuities does not correspond to a real phenomenon.[16]

3.4 The Failure of Mean-Field Theories: When More Is Different

We now turn our attention to continuous phase transitions. One of the first attempts to explain the occurrence of this type of phase transition was Landau

---

[15] A similar point was made by Bangu (2009, 2015).

[16] For a philosophical discussion on finite approaches to first-order phase transitions, see Ardourel (2018).

theory, which is a phenomenological theory that does not include the elementary degrees of freedom of the statistical model. In this theory, which can also be considered a "mean-field theory," the free energy is written as a function of the *order parameter*, which is a quantity with zero value in the $T > T_c$ *unbroken symmetry state* and nonzero value in the $T < T_c$ *broken symmetry state* (see Section 2.4). For a magnet, the order parameter is the magnetization and in the liquid–gas transition is the density.

In Landau theory, the Landau free energy $F(M)$ is derived from symmetry considerations alone, and thermal equilibrium is reached when the free energy takes a minimum value. Since this theory uses only the symmetry properties of the free energy $F(M)$, it is predicted that the critical exponents depend neither on the spatial dimensionality nor on the number of spin components (e.g. the Ising model has one-spin component). However, this independence of dimensionality and number of spin components proved to be incorrect and the values of the critical exponents, which were the same as the values of the mean-field approximation, were shown to be wrong.[17]

So, although Landau theory and the mean-field theory could successfully describe the qualitative and quantitative behavior outside of the critical region (Kadanoff, 2009, 2010; Nishimori and Ortiz, 2010), they both fail to accurately predict the behavior of critical phenomena for dimension $d \leq 4$. The reason is that they are valid only when fluctuations around the average of physical quantities are approximately negligible, and critical phenomena are governed by fluctuations. In fact, one can derive a condition of fluctuations to prove the internal consistency of mean-field theories, including Landau theory. This condition is called *Ginzburg criterion* and can be written as follows:

$$T(T_c - T)^{-\gamma} << (T_c - T)^{2\beta}(T_c - T)^{-\nu d}, \qquad (3.15)$$

where β, γ, and ν are the critical exponents associated in magnetic materials, respectively, to magnetization, magnetic susceptibility, and correlation length, and d is the dimension. Since the mean-field theory as well as Landau theory predict values $\gamma = 1, \beta = \nu = 1/2$, this implies that $d > 4$. This means that near and at the critical point the mean-field theory will work only for dimension $d > 4$, and the theory is expected to fail qualitatively and quantitatively for $d \leq 4$. The theory could also not explain the occurrence of universality, which is characteristic of critical phenomena.

---

[17] In fact, the experimental values of the critical exponents for magnetic materials were observed to be approximately $\gamma = 1.233, \beta = 0.341$, and $\nu = 0.62$. In contrast, Landau theory and mean-field theories predicted values of $\gamma = 1, \beta = 1/2$, and $\nu = 1/2$ (Nishimori and Ortiz, 2010, p. 46).

The small discrepancy between the experimental values of the critical exponents and the values predicted by the mean-field theories was, as Goldenfeld (1992, p. 16) puts it, "the tip of a well-hidden iceberg." In fact, the failure of mean-field theories close to the critical point, more than the failure of a specific approximation method, is a beautiful demonstration of *cooperative behavior*, which implies that the aggregate behavior close to a continuous phase transition cannot be extrapolated from the behavior of a small number of particles, at least on the basis of conventional statistical mechanics. The reason for this is that, close to the critical point, fluctuations with different sizes dominate the behavior and have correlations that persist over distances comparable to the correlation length ξ. In general, how much we can reduce the size of the system without changing its main properties depends on the correlation length ξ, which measures the distance over which the particles are correlated. In favorable circumstances such as the cases examined in Sections 3.2 and 3.3, the correlation length is only a few atomic spacings. The main problem of critical phenomena is that near the critical point, the correlation length ξ is very large and becomes conceptually infinite at the critical point (Wilson and Kogut, 1974). The divergence of the correlation length is then responsible for the failure of standard approximations such as mean-field theories and requires the use of RG methods, which will be examined in Section 4. The failure of mean-field theory suggests that the behavior of a system with many degrees of freedom at the critical point is qualitatively novel with respect to the behavior of a system with only a few degrees of freedom. This is the reason why most philosophers (e.g. Butterfield, 2011b; Norton, 2014) and physicists (e.g. Anderson, 1972; Wilson and Kogut, 1974) agree that critical phenomena are an instance of emergent behavior.

In Section 3.1, we characterized few-many emergence on the basis of five properties, including epistemological novelty, which means that the global behavior of the many-particle system can neither be explained nor predicted by studying the behavior of a fairly small number of components. The failure of mean-field theories to predict and adequately explain universality and, more generally, the behavior close to the critical point suggests that the behavior of a system undergoing a critical phase transition is *epistemologically emergent* with respect to the behavior of small samples of it, and therefore that this is a case of *few-many emergence*.

One may also argue that the behavior of a system undergoing a continuous phase transitions is *ontologically emergent* with respect to the behavior of a few components. In fact, a real behavior, namely a critical phase transition, seems to arise only when there are fluctuations that persist over distances comparable to the correlation length, which is usually very large and even conceptually infinite at the critical point, and this cannot occur in small systems. However, in the past decades, physicists have developed alternative approaches to phase transitions for nonextensive systems that allow for a definition of continuous phase transitions for very small systems, for instance, in terms of the topology of the micro-canonical entropy function (Gross, 2001; Gross and Votyakov, 2000). It is not clear, however, whether the phase transitions observed in such small nonextensive systems are of the same kind as the ones observed in larger systems, which are governed by fluctuations (Gross and Votyakov, 2000).

Independent of whether the behavior characterizing a phase transition is ontologically "few-many emergent" or only epistemologically "few-many emergent," this seems to be a case of "weak" rather than "strong emergence," since it is assumed that the big system is constituted by the same kind of degrees of freedom and governed by the same fundamental laws as small samples of it. We will come back to this in Section 4.5, when we discuss microphysicalism. Finally, the behavior close to the critical point is also robust since it does not depend on the behavior of specific components. The robustness of critical behavior is also demonstrated by the use of RG methods, which will be addressed in Section 4. In sum, critical phenomena seem to display all the features that we used to characterize "few-many emergence." It is therefore not surprising that they are a prime example of Anderson's "More Is Different" thesis.

3.5 Concluding Remarks

In this section, we have analyzed the notion of "few-many emergence" and correspondingly "few-many reduction" by focusing on a few case studies from physics. We also contrasted this type of emergence with the notion of "parts-whole emergence." In spite of the use of the thermodynamic limit, we argued that first-order phase transitions are a successful case of few-many reduction, since mean-field theories give us a qualitative understanding of the phenomena on the basis of the behavior of a few particles. However, we argued that continuous phase transitions are better understood as case of "few-many emergence." This is because fluctuations, which extend over distances much larger than the atomic spacing, dominate the behavior close to the critical point. This implies, at least from the perspective of conventional statistical mechanics, that the global behavior of the many-particle system cannot be understood by focusing on the behavior of systems with a small number of components. We argued that this is also the reason why mean-field theories fail to give accurate predictions for this behavior. Similar behavior is displayed by the binding of large molecules, the "Kondo" behavior (a magnetic impurity in a metal) and cooperative phenomena in general (Wilson and Kogut, 1974).

The failure of mean-field theories to predict the accurate values of the critical exponents motivated the development of the RG approach. In the next section, we will analyze the main aspects of this approach and we will explain how the RG approach can successfully account for critical behavior and universality. The use of RG methods leads to a different notion of emergence that I will call "coarse-grained emergence," which is associated with the autonomy and novelty of coarse-grained descriptions. This notion of "coarse-grained emergence" needs to be distinguished from the notion of "few-many emergence" not only because the scales that we consider in the two cases are different, but also because the relevant notion of novelty differs in these two types of emergence.

4 Universality, Renormalization, and Effective (-field) Theories

Until about fifty years ago, there was no physical theory that allowed one both to predict the accurate values of the critical exponents governing a critical phase transition for dimension $d \leq 4$ and to explain universality, that is, the intriguing fact that different physical systems such as liquids and ferromagnets share the same set of critical exponents (Sections 2 and 3).[18] An explanation of the discrepancy between experiments and mean-field theories as well as an explanation of universality was first given by Kenneth Wilson in a series of seminal papers published in 1971, where he developed the central ideas of the RG approach.

The development of RG methods and the explanation of universality gave Kenneth Wilson the Nobel Prize in physics in 1982 and suggested a new way of looking at physics, which had an impact not only in condensed matter physics and high-energy physics but also in the philosophy of physics. In this section, we will explain the main aspects of the Wilsonian approach and will develop a concept of emergence that suits this framework. This concept of emergence will also serve to characterize emergence for a class of EFTs. I will end this section with some remarks on the "reductive character" of RG explanations.

4.1 Wilsonian Renormalization

For Wilson and Kogut (1974), the RG approach has two main objectives. The first is to simplify the task of solving systems with many degrees of

---

[18] Previously, series expansions were used to determine the values of critical exponents with accurate results, but they were incapable of explaining the phenomenon of universality (Fisher, 1974).

freedom contained within a large correlation length as the case of critical phase transitions examined in Sections 2 and 3. The second is to explain how qualitative features of cooperative behavior arise, which is also related with giving an explanation of universal behavior. Based on previous ideas developed by Kadanoff (1996) mentioned in Section 2.3, Wilson suggested a very progressive method in which one successively coarse-grains the effective degrees of freedom of the system by means of a series of transformations, R, with the hope that the transformation will eventually reach out for information about the parts of the system that are (infinitely) far away, without having to calculate the partition function exactly. For each transformation, there are two basic steps. The first is to coarse-grain the description of the microscopic system. The second is to rescale basic variables such as lengths to try to restore the original picture (see Figure 7). The core idea then is to analyze how the coupling constants in the effective Hamiltonian change under a change of scale and a rescaling of the degrees of freedom.

There are two main kinds of RG methods:

- *Real-space RG*, which is applied to discrete systems on a lattice in real space.
- *Momentum* (*k-space*) *RG*, which is essentially field-theoretic RG and is applied to continuous systems in momentum (or Fourier) space.

We will examine these two types of RG methods next.

4.1.1 Real-Space RG

In real-space RG, the coarse-graining operations are performed on a discrete set of lattice spin sites. Although the procedure is general, it is practical to illustrate the main ideas of real-space RG with the example of block spin transformations in the Ising model. As we said before, the number of degrees of freedom that are mutually correlated is proportional to the correlation length ξ. As the system approaches the critical temperature, ξ tends to infinity, which means that the number of degrees of freedom also tends to infinity. In order to deal with this problem, which was also mentioned in Section 3.4, RG methods seek to successively reduce the number of effective degrees of freedom and in this way reduce the effective correlation length. One way of achieving this is by grouping the spins of a lattice with spacing a into blocks of length ba, where $b > 1$ is called the *scaling factor* (see Figure 7). One can then replace the spins within a block of side ba by a single *block spin* that contains b^d spins, where d is the lattice dimension. In this process, one reduces the total number of degrees of freedom from N to $N' = N/b^d$.

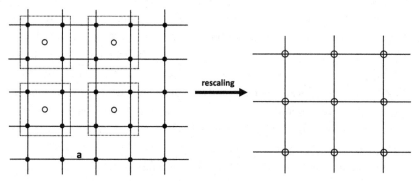

Figure 7 Representation of block-spin transformation. The blocks (groups of four spins) behave as if they were single-block spins. At each coarse-graining step, the number of effective degrees of freedom is reduced

Let us now examine this coarse-graining procedure in more detail. We define a block spin S'_I in block I by:

$$S'_I = f(S_i), \tag{4.1}$$

where f stands for "majority rule" or "decimation" and S_i are the spins of the original lattice. One assumes that there must exist a Hamiltonian $H'[S'_I]$ such that the probability of observing a configuration $[S'_I]$ is given by:

$$P[S'_I] \sim exp\{-\beta H'[S'_I]\}. \tag{4.2}$$

After following a series of simple steps (details in McComb, 2004), one can demonstrate that the partition function of the system must remain (approximately) invariant under the RG transformation, that is:

$$Z = \sum_{[S_i]} exp\{-\beta H[S_i]\} = \sum_{[S'_I]} exp\{-\beta H'[S'_I]\} = Z'. \tag{4.3}$$

The invariance of the partition function also implies the invariance of the free energy and therefore assures that the relevant physical properties of the system remain in the coarse-graining description. It is important to note that, in contrast to what Kadanoff assumed, there is no reason to expect that the Hamiltonian should remain unchanged under the application of the RG transformation. In fact, new local operators can be generated during the RG transformation. Correspondingly, the change of the original Hamiltonian H under the application of a transformation R_b can be written as:

$$H' = R_b(H), \tag{4.4}$$

where R_b is the RG transformation.

The RG strategy then consists of iterating R_b many times until we trace out all irrelevant short-range fluctuations and we can shift our attention to the long-length behavior of the system. The hope is that an unbounded repetition of this coarse-graining process will reveal the critical behavior of the system, allowing us to calculate the critical exponents and to explain universality. As we will see next, the existence of nontrivial fixed points plays a crucial role in the achievement of these goals. In fact, if the original system is at the critical point, the system will have fluctuations of all length scales and will eventually remain unchanged after many iterations of the RG transformation. This is a consequence of the *scale invariance* explained in Section 2.3, which refers here to the invariance of the Hamiltonian under the group of scale transformations (Cao and Schweber, 1993).

When the Hamiltonian does not change any more by applying a transformation, we say that we have reached a *fixed point*. Formally, the fixed point is defined by:

$$H^* = R_b(H^*). \tag{4.5}$$

Since the correlation length diverges at the critical point, usually infinitely many steps are required to reach a nontrivial fixed point. This means that the fixed point H^* is reached asymptotically when the number of iterations n of the RG transformation goes to infinity (Nishimori and Ortiz, 2010).

$$H^* = \lim_{n \to \infty} R_b^n(H_c), \tag{4.6}$$

where H_c is the original Hamiltonian at the critical point. The limit $n \to \infty$, which I call the "the infinite iteration limit," will play an important role in the discussion on inter-theory reduction in Section 5.4.

The changes in the Hamiltonian can be represented by a flow in the Hamiltonian space (or parameter space) that defines a *semi-group* (and not a group), in which information is erased irreversibly as one traces out degrees of freedom. This means that there is no inverse transformation.

One can also understand this process in terms of the set of coupling constants $[K]$, which are the external parameters, such as field exchange interaction parameters, temperature, and so on, associated with the effective Hamiltonians. In this case, the fixed point in the coupling constant space is defined as:

$$[K^*] = R_b[K^*]. \tag{4.7}$$

Apart from nontrivial fixed points, it is possible to arrive at trivial fixed points, namely $K = 0$ and $K = \infty$, which correspond to the low- and high-temperature fixed points, respectively.

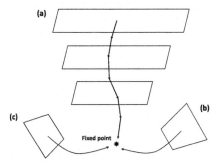

Figure 8 Representation of different members of the same universality class flowing toward a nontrivial fixed point (adapted from Fisher, 1998)

For any set of coupling constants one can compute the correlation length, which is transformed under R_b according to:

$$\xi[K'] = \xi[K]/b. \tag{4.8}$$

This means that the effective correlation length is reduced in every step by the factor b. After n iterations of the RG transformation, the correlation length changes according to:

$$\xi[K] = b\xi[K^{(1)}] = b^2\xi[K^{(2)}] = \ldots = b^n\xi[K^{(n)}]. \tag{4.9}$$

Since the goal of RG methods is to reduce the effective correlation length until the effective degrees of freedom are of the order of the original correlation length, the previous expression implies that if the system has originally a large correlation length, the number of iterations of the RG transformation should be large. Correspondingly, if the original correlation length is infinite, one has to take the limit $n \to \infty$ at the right-hand side of Eq. (4.9).

The RG approach gives an explanation of universality by showing that systems that behave in the same way at the critical point, flow toward the same nontrivial fixed-point. The original Hamiltonians that flow toward the same nontrivial fixed point are said to be in the *basin of attraction* of the critical point and are said to belong to the same *universality class* (see Figure 8). For instance, the three-dimensional Ising model, the liquid–gas critical transition, and the ferromagnetic–paramagnetic transition, all belong to the same universality class.

The fact that different Hamiltonians flow toward the same fixed point is, then, the basic mechanism for universality and has motivated interesting discussions on emergence that will be examined later in this section.

Apart from giving an explanation of universality, the RG approach allows one to calculate the critical exponents, which can be determined by analyzing the behavior of the RG flows near a nontrivial fixed point. More specifically, one can linearize the RG transformation about a fixed point by considering only infinitesimal variations. To do this, one starts by setting Hamiltonians that are infinitesimally close to the fixed point, for example:

$$K_n = K_n^* + \delta K_n, K_n' = K_n^* + \delta K_n', \tag{4.10}$$

and then "Taylor expand" the RG transformation around the fixed point such that:

$$\delta K_n' = A_b(K_n^*) \delta K_n, \tag{4.11}$$

where the matrix $A_b(K_n^*)$ is given by:

$$A_b(K^*) = \left[\frac{\delta K_n'}{\delta K_n} \right]_{K_n^*}. \tag{4.12}$$

The eigenvalue λ_i of this matrix allow us to evaluate critical exponents and to establish relations among them (details in Goldenfeld, 1992; McComb, 2004). Moreover, they tell us what components of the vector $[\delta K]$ (scaling fields) grow or shrink under the RG transformation. One can distinguish between three types of variables:

- *Relevant variables:* $|\lambda_i| > 1$, which grow as b increases, moving the trajectory away from the critical point, and therefore away from the nontrivial fixed point.
- *Irrelevant variables:* $|\lambda_i| < 1$, which shrink as b increases, moving the trajectory in the direction of the nontrivial fixed point.
- *Marginal variables:* $|\lambda_i| = 0$, which do not change as b increases.

In the case of a ferromagnet, the relevant variables are temperature T and the external magnetic field h. In fact, critical behavior is observed only when these parameters are adjusted as $T = T_c$ and $h = 0$ and any slight deviation from these values will drive the system away from the critical point by RG operations. These quantities are therefore non-universal variables. Interestingly, properties other than temperature or external field can be shown to be irrelevant or marginal, meaning that they have no influence on the critical exponents. In fact, it can be proven that critical behavior depends only on the spatial dimension and the symmetries of the original Hamiltonians and not on the strength of the nonlinear couplings or other nonuniversal parameters.

The aforementioned text means that the entire description of the behavior of the system has been reduced to the properties of the neighborhood of the nontrivial fixed point. In other words, the RG approach shows that the behavior of critical phenomena is independent of the details that characterize the system away from the nontrivial fixed point. We will see next that this also implies that the critical behavior is *robust* with respect to microscopic details.

4.1.2 Momentum-Space RG

Momentum-space (k-space) RG is analogous to real-space RG, but here one integrates out high-wave modes from a continuous spin field instead of performing operations on a discrete lattice. One then rescales the coarse-grained field. The space here is momentum space, which is conjugate to real space.[19] A distinctive property of k-space RG is the role of the dimensionality of the field as a control parameter, which allows one to calculate a nontrivial fixed point for $d = 4 - \epsilon$ and thus to correct mean-field values (Wilson and Kogut, 1974). The justification for going from a discrete description to a continuous description in the study of critical phenomena is that when the system approaches the critical point, fluctuations have large spatial extension and, therefore, the fine structure of the lattice can be smeared out into a continuum. This means that if the system is near the critical point, there is an equivalence between the continuum version of the theory and the lattice version. One can then measure the distance from some origin as a continuously varying coordinate, instead of measuring distance in terms of a discrete number of unit cells.

Let us review this process in some detail. The starting point of k-space RG is to make a transition from a description based on discrete particles to one based on continuous fields, by taking the *continuum limit* $N \rightarrow \infty$. In order to do that, one writes the discrete spins as a discretization of a continuous function $S(x)$, that is:

$$S_i = S(x_i). \tag{4.13}$$

One then introduces a coarse-graining transformation such that:

$$S^{(D)}(x_i) \rightarrow \phi(x), \tag{4.14}$$

where the D-component spin vector on a d-dimensional lattice becomes the D-component field on a d-dimensional space (details in McComb, 2004). This means that one averages $S^{(D)}(x_i)$ over a volume $(ba)^b$, where b is of the order of a few lattice spaces and $ba << \xi$.

Interestingly, in contrast to quantum field theory, there is an ultraviolet *cutoff* on the permitted wave number values $|k|$, such that:

$$|k| \leq \Lambda \sim \pi/a, \tag{4.15}$$

which means that the cutoff is due to the lattice constant a. The RG transformation involves successively decreasing the cutoff (decreasing the energy), thereby increasing the minimum scale of fluctuations considered.

---

[19] This takes us into quantum field theory, but the Planck constant is taken to be unity.

In order to make the transition to wave number space, one introduces the Fourier transform of the field:

$$\phi(x) = \int_{0 \le k \le \Lambda} \frac{d^d k}{(2\pi)^d} exp\{i\mathbf{k} \cdot \mathbf{x}\}\phi(\mathbf{k}), \tag{4.16}$$

in d dimensions.

In general, the transition from microscopic to continuum descriptions requires the introduction of densities, which are functionals (i.e. functions of functions) of the field $\phi(x)$. The Hamiltonian density h can be defined such that:

$$H = \int d^d x h. \tag{4.17}$$

The associated partition functional becomes:

$$Z = \int \mathcal{D}\phi(x) exp\{-\beta \int d^d x h(\phi(x))\}, \tag{4.18}$$

where $\int \mathcal{D}\phi(x)$ can be interpreted as "sum over states."

The most important steps in k-space RG can then be summarized as follows (McComb, 2004):

1. We integrate over modes in the band of wave numbers:

$$\Lambda/b \le k \le \Lambda. \tag{4.19}$$

2. Rescale the system in real space, that is:

$$x \rightarrow x/b = x'; \tag{4.20}$$

$$\int d^d x \rightarrow \int b^d d^d x = \int d^d x'. \tag{4.21}$$

3. Rescale the system in wave number space, that is:

$$k \rightarrow bk = k'; \tag{4.22}$$

$$\int d^d k \rightarrow \int b^d d^d k = \int d^d k'. \tag{4.23}$$

One then calculates the critical exponents in an analogous way as in real-space RG, namely by expansions near the critical nontrivial fixed points. An advantage of k-space RG is that, as mentioned earlier, one can "cure" the problems of mean-field theory for $d < 4$ by expanding in Taylor series about $d = 4$ in powers of ϵ, which gives a theory in $d = 4 - \epsilon$. This method was proposed by Wilson and Kogut (1974) and is known as the "ϵ-expansion."[20]

---

[20] See Franklin (2018) for a philosophical comparison between momentum-space and real-space RG.

It is important to point out that in contrast to other renormalization approaches such as the Gell–Man–Low approach (Novikov et al., 1983), in which RG transformations are deducible a priori from scale dependence of parameters, in the Wilsonian renormalization approach there is no standard "recipe" for designing RG transformations and one generally needs external guidance coming partially from an empirical investigation of the system to distinguish between couplings of least importance and those of most importance. As Fisher (1998, p. 672) puts it: "The design of effective RG transformations turns out to be an art more than a science: there is no standard recipe!"[21]

4.2 The Robustness/Universality Distinction

The success of RG methods to calculate the critical exponents near the critical point and to explain universality has led to the most exciting discussions on emergent behavior in physics. However, in order to understand the extent to which universal behavior is "emergent," one needs to distinguish between two notions that tend to be conflated in the philosophical literature, namely *robustness* and *universality*. Robustness should be understood as insensitivity of some behavior to variation of the microphysical details that characterize a particular token (e.g. instances of different ultraviolet physics underlying the occurrence of phase transitions in ferromagnets) (Gryb et al., 2020). This means that a behavior observed in a particular type of system is robust if it is invariant upon different perturbations involving changes in the microscopic details of that system. On the other hand, universality should be interpreted as insensitivity of some behavior to variation of the macroscopic details that characterize the type of system considered. In other words, a behavior is universal if it remains invariant upon changes in the type of system under investigation, such as fluids, ferromagnets, and antiferromagnets.

The beauty of RG methods is that they show that critical behavior is both robust and universal. Indeed, although it imposes some restrictions regarding the type of possible micro-interactions, for example it requires the interactions to be short-range and expressible in terms of a convergent set of constraints (Wilson and Kogut, 1974), it shows that the behavior near the critical point only depends on the symmetries of the original Hamiltonian and the spatial dimension and not on any other microscopic detail. As already stated, this

---

[21] This issue has led some physicists and philosophers (e.g. Bain, 2013a, 2013b; Cao and Schweber, 1993) to defend an antireductionist interpretation of RG methods. However, I will argue in Sections 4.3, 4.4, and 5.5 that this should be rather taken as an argument to disentangle the notion of reduction from the possibility of deducing coarse-grained from fine-grained descriptions without external guidance.

is established by the existence of a nontrivial fixed point, which allows for the calculation of the critical exponents without having to take into account micro-physical details. Moreover, the same theoretical framework allows for an explanation of universality, in the sense that it shows that the systems that behave in the same way close to the critical point flow toward the same nontrivial fixed point. In other words, it proves that the details that distinguish different types of systems within the same universality class do not matter for the occurrence of critical behavior (Batterman 2005, 2019).

It is important to point out, however, that universality and robustness do not necessarily come together. In fact, one may find a behavior that is universal in the sense that it is invariant under inter-type variations, but not robust in the sense that it depends on micro-physical details. Correspondingly, one may find behavior that is robust in the sense that it is independent on microphysical details but not universal, since it is highly type-specific (Gryb et al., 2020). Proving that a certain behavior is both robust and universal can be crucial to derive an autonomous description of the phenomenon that does not depend on the micro-physical details and at the same time can be used to describe the same behavior in different types of systems. Indeed, establishing that a certain behavior is both robust and universal usually constitutes the first step toward the construction of a coarse-grained description of the system that captures everything that is physically relevant without having to take into account micro-physical details (e.g. ultra-short wavelengths, high energy effects). We will see next that these coarse-grained or effective descriptions are not only pragmatically useful (it is often easier to perform calculations in coarse-grained models than in fined-grained models), but they can also be essential to understand some physical behavior, especially when the microphysics (e.g. high-energy physics) is unknown.

4.3 Emergence of Coarse-Grained Descriptions

From what has been said here, one can distinguish an interesting notion of emergence associated with the use of RG methods. This notion of emergence is different from the notion of "few-many emergence" discussed in Section 3. Indeed, in this case, one does not compare the behavior of the many-particle system with small samples of it, but rather a fine-grained description of the entire system with coarse-grained descriptions of the same system, which result from applying an RG transformation many (or infinitely many!) times. In other words, in the RG approach we are interested in comparing the behavior of the entire many-particle system at different levels of description (i.e. fine-grained and coarse-grained levels).

I will call the notion of emergence involved in autonomous coarse-grained descriptions "coarse-grained emergence" in order to distinguish it from the notion of "few-many emergence" discussed in Section 3. Coarse-grained emergence can be defined as follows:

> **Coarse-grained emergence:** A coarse-grained description of a system emerges *synchronically* upon a fine-grained description, iff the former has terms denoting properties or behavior that are *novel* and *autonomous* with respect to the latter, and these properties or behavior *supervene* upon the behavior of the components of the fine-grained description.

Let us outline the features of this type of emergence in more detail.

(i) *The fine-grained/coarse-grained distinction:* Here one distinguishes between fine-grained descriptions, which describe the system at a high-energy scale/small length scale and a series of coarse-grained descriptions that can result from coarse-graining operations, which describe the system at a lower-energy scale/larger length scale.

(ii) *Novelty:* Novelty means here that the coarse-grained description has features that are not features of the fine-grained description. In other words, the coarse-grained description is formally and conceptually distinct from the fine-grained theory and has terms (i.e. coupling constants, degrees of freedom) that do not appear in the fine-grained description (Bain, 2013b; Crowther, 2015). Moreover, the coarse-grained description may describe a behavior that cannot be predicted or explained solely on the basis of the fine-grained theory (Batterman 2005, 2011, 2019).

(iii) *Synchronic:* The behavior represented by the fine-grained description exists at the same time as the behavior represented by the coarse-grained description.

(iv) *Autonomy:* A coarse-grained description is *strongly* autonomous with respect to a fine-grained description iff it describes a behavior that is both robust and universal. A coarse-grained description is *weakly* autonomous with respect to a fine-grained description iff it describes a behavior that is either robust or universal, but not both.

(v) *Robustness:* The coarse-grained description refers to some behavior that is insensitive to variation of the microphysical details that characterize a particular token (Gryb et al., 2020).

(vi) *Universality:* The coarse-grained description refers to some behavior that is insensitive to variation of the macroscopic details that characterize the type of system considered (Gryb et al., 2020). This is close to the philosophical notion of "multiple realizability" (cf. Batterman, 2001, pp. 73–76).

(vii) *Supervenience:* The coarse-grained level depends on the fine-grained
level in the sense that it supervenes upon it (Crowther, 2015). Supervenience means in this context that every change in the coarse-grained level
must imply a change in the fine-grained level, but the converse does not
hold. Correspondingly, two systems that are the same according to the
fine-grained description should also be the same according to the coarse-
grained description, provided that the RG transformation is the same. We
will see next that this also assures that the coarse-grained behavior is ultimately constituted by the same components present in the fine-grained
description, which means that microphysicalism is secured (Bain, 2013b;
Mainwood, 2006).

If we associate this definition of coarse-grained emergence with the distinctions drawn in Section 1.1, we can say that this type of emergence is *weak*,
since it is compatible with microphysicalism (we will give arguments in this
direction in Section 4.5), usually *epistemological*, since typically the kind of
novelty at stake is a property of our description of the system rather than of the
system itself,[22] and *synchronic*, because we are interested in comparing two
levels of description that describe the system at the same time.

Before placing this discussion in the context of effective (-field) theories,
I will explain why this definition of emergence applies to the case of critical
behavior.

We have seen in Section 4.1 that in the Wilsonian framework, one coarse-
grains the degrees of freedom of the original Hamiltonian by means of a
transformation and repeats this process many times until all irrelevant details
are traced out. In other words, one studies how the coupling constants in the
effective Hamiltonians change under an increase in the length scale (or decrease
of the cutoff Λ). The calculation of the critical exponents and the explanation
of universal behavior are then given by an unbounded repetition of this coarse-
graining procedure which results in a nontrivial fixed point. This means that
in the Wilsonian explanation of critical behavior, one actually compares the
behavior of fine-grained with coarse-grained descriptions, so that property (i)
of coarse-grained emergence is satisfied.

The use of RG methods to explain critical phenomena also satisfies condition (ii) of coarse-grained descriptions. Indeed, the coarse-grained description
represented by a nontrivial fixed point $H^* = R_b(H^*)$ is *novel* with respect to the

---

[22] This does not rule out the possibility of interpreting coarse-grained emergence in an ontological
sense, but to do so, one would need further arguments suggesting that the coarse-grained description refers to real properties, which are ontologically distinct from the properties of fine-grained
descriptions.

fine-grained description given by the original Hamiltonian H_c, because the set of coupling constants K^* and the effective degrees of freedom of the coarse-grained Hamiltonian H^* differ from those present in the original Hamiltonian H_c. In fact, as we saw in Section 4.1, until a fixed point is reached, every coarse-graining transformation R_b changes the set of coupling constants according to $K' = R_b(K)$ in real-space renormalization and analogously in momentum-space renormalization, in which one integrates over modes of wave numbers. These changes in the Hamiltonian (or Lagrangian) can be represented in both approaches by a flow in the Hamiltonian (or Lagrangian) space, which implies that there are "novel terms" in the coarse-grained descriptions with respect to the fine-grained description.

There is yet another sense in which critical phenomena are novel with respect to specific fine-grained descriptions, namely universal behavior cannot be explained solely on the basis of the fine-grained description of an individual system. In this sense, the RG approach, which coarse-grains the system, appears to be ineliminable (Batterman, 2005, 2011; Menon and Callender, 2011). To illustrate this, imagine that we could solve the 3D Ising model exactly. Such a detailed derivation may allow us to predict the critical exponents for systems in the same universality class, but would not allow us to explain why different types of systems display the same behavior. This is because an explanation of universality requires abstracting away the irrelevant information that is type-specific and retaining only the factors that are relevant to characterize critical behavior in different systems. Knox (2016), for instance, points out that although abstraction is not the whole story in the explanation of universality (idealizations also play an important role), it is mainly due to abstraction that the RG approach allows one to explain the fact that different systems behave in the same way close to the critical point.

The question of whether such abstract explanations of universality are reducible to the microphysical description or not has been a matter of controversy in the philosophical literature. Batterman (2005, 2011, 2019), for instance, has used the apparent need for coarse-grained descriptions in the explanation of universality to motivate an antireductionist view of critical phase transitions.[23] Franklin (2019), on the other hand, has argued that although the RG approach plays an ineliminable role in the explanation of universality, it is possible to reduce the RG explanation to the microphysical description by considering the common features shared by all the members of a universality

---

[23] Another argument used by Batterman for the irreducibility of critical phase transitions is the apparent need for infinite limits in the RG approach. We will address this argument in Section 5.2.

class and scale invariance, which is, for him, a physical phenomenon that can be microphysically explained. In Section 5.4, I will give different arguments in favor of the reduction of RG explanations, but for now it is important to emphasize that the type of "explanatory novelty" of coarse-grain descriptions that I was arguing for is not incompatible with Franklin's view. In fact, what I claim to be irreducible is not the RG explanation to microphysical descriptions or fine-grained descriptions, but rather the explanation of universality to fine-grained descriptions without invoking the coarse-graining procedure attached to the RG approach. Since Franklin also recognizes the ineliminable role of the RG methods in the explanation of universality, he seems to agree with this "irreducible" aspect in the explanation of universality.[24]

It is also easy to see that this approach satisfies conditions (v) and (vi). In fact, in the RG approach, the *robustness* of critical behavior is established by the disappearance of the irrelevant couplings as one increases the length scale, or in the momentum-space approach, as one decreases the cutoff. In other words, one shows that the critical behavior associated to a single type of systems depends only on the spatial dimension and the symmetries of the original Hamiltonians and not on the strength of the nonlinear couplings or other non-universal parameters. Simultaneously, by showing that the Hamiltonians of all systems that exhibit identical behavior at the critical point flow toward the same nontrivial fixed point, this framework successfully establishes the *universality* of that behavior. In other words, one proves that the behavior that characterizes critical phase transitions is insensitive to an inter-type variation within the members of the universality class.

Since the RG approach serves to demonstrate both the universality and robustness of critical behavior, it serves to establish the *autonomy* (in the strong sense) of the coarse-grained description represented by nontrivial fixed points. This means that the fixed-point Hamiltonian gives an autonomous description of critical behavior that is robust upon microscopic details and that can also be used to characterize the behavior of other systems within the same universality class. This means that condition (iv) is also satisfied.

Finally, the RG explanation of critical phenomena also serves to establish the *supervenience* of the behavior observed at the coarse-grained level upon the behavior of the components that are present in the fine-grained description

---

[24] There is an interesting discussion in the philosophical literature regarding the character of RG explanations. For many, RG explanations are a prototypical example of noncausal explanations (e.g. Batterman and Rice, 2014; Reutlinger, 2014), while others (Sullivan, 2019) are critical of this view. A detailed discussion on the type of explanation associated with the RG approach goes beyond the scope of this Element.

(condition vii). This is because the RG approach has a particular direction in the process of coarse-graining, in which larger length scales can be shown to depend (in a minimal sense) on smaller length scales, but not vice versa (Crowther, 2015). This dependency is warranted by the existence of a transformation R_b that coarse-grains the degrees of freedom of the fine-grained description in the real-space renormalization, and, respectively, by an RG transformation that integrates out the degrees of freedom in the momentum-space renormalization. This means that, in this framework, the effective degrees of freedom of the coarse-grained description are ultimately constituted by the degrees of freedom of the fine-grained description. In other words, if two fine-grained descriptions are identical, they will lead to the same coarse-grained description, provided that the coarse-graining transformation is the same. Correspondingly, a change in the coarse-grained description will be associated with a change in the behavior of degrees of freedom of the fine-grained description, if the coarse-graining transformation is the same. This dependency of the coarse-grained description on the fine-grained description also serves to secure *microphysicalism* and is the reason why coarse-grained emergence is *weak* rather than *strong*, despite the explanatory novelty associated with the explanation of universality.

4.4 Emergence and Effective Field Theories

Georgi (1993) says:

> one of the most astonishing aspects of the world is that there seems to be interesting physics at all scales. Whenever we look in a previously unexplored regime of distance, time or energy, we find new physical phenomena. [...] To do physics amid this remarkable richness, it is convenient to be able to isolate a set of phenomena from all the rest, so that we can describe it without having to understand everything. (pp. 3–4)

These appropriate descriptions of the relevant physics at a given scale that Georgi is referring to are EFTs. Huggett and Weingard (1995) define an "Effective Field Theory" as a theory that "effectively captures everything relevant [at a given scale]" (p. 172).

Usually, EFTs are constructed through a process in which the degrees of freedom are eliminated (or integrated out) from a high-energy or short length scale theory (Bain, 2013b). In this sense, the coarse-grained Hamiltonian (or Lagrangian) that accounts for critical behavior in the RG framework is a prime example of an EFT. However, the theory of critical behavior is by no means the only example of EFTs in physics. To the contrary, EFTs play an essential role in many different areas of physics, ranging from particle physics and condensed matter physics to inflationary cosmology. Furthermore, it is common among physicists to think of all our current physical theories, including the Standard Model, as low-energy EFTs of some unknown fundamental theory (Luu and Meißner, 2019; Rivat and Grinbaum, 2020)

The type of behavior that can be described by an EFT has often been regarded as "emergent." Philosophers and physicists have presented different accounts of emergence associated with EFTs (e.g. Bain, 2013a, 2013b; Butterfield, 2014; Cao and Schweber, 1993; Crowther, 2015; Ellis, 2020; Hartmann, 2001; Luu and Meißner, 2019; Mainwood, 2006). I will now focus on some of these accounts and I will argue that the notion of "coarse-grained emergence" developed in the previous sections can serve to characterize at least a set of EFTs.

There are two main approaches to EFT. The first is "bottom-up," which means going from low-energy EFTs ("bottom") to high-energy EFTs ("up").[25] More precisely, one constructs an effective higher-energy theory with cutoff Λ_2 on the basis of a well-known lower energy theory with cutoff Λ_1, where $\Lambda_2 > \Lambda_1$. This approach requires adding new terms (coupling-constants) in order to account for high-energy effects (details in Crowther, 2015; Hartmann, 2001; Manohar and Wise, 2007). The second is the "top-down" approach that consists in constructing a low-energy theory on the basis of a high-energy theory, which can be done by using "matching conditions" that assure that the relevant physics remain in the low-energy level (large length scale) description (a process known as the *continuum EFT*), or by integrating out the high energy (short length scale) interactions, which corresponds to the Wilsonian approach (Bain, 2013a, 2013b; Crowther, 2015; Georgi, 1993; Huggett and Weingard, 1995).

In the "bottom-up" approach, the higher energy effective theory is usually constructed by identifying the relevant symmetries of the phenomenon and by a local operator expansion that includes all possible interactions consistent with these symmetries. An example of the bottom-up approach is the standard model of particle physics. The standard model encompasses the strong quantum chromodynamics (QCD), weak and electromagnetic (QED) interactions, but can be considered incomplete since it does not include gravity. Assuming that interesting physics may occur at the Planck energy scale 1.2×10^{25} MeV (and even before), the standard model itself is usually considered a low-energy EFT. In order to construct a higher-energy EFT on the basis of the standard model, one

---

[25] Note that "bottom-up/top-down" refers here to energy scales: high-energy scales are the "high level" and low-energy scales are the "low level." This can lead to confusion, since in the philosophical discussion around emergence the order of levels is generally inverted.

should identify the relevant symmetries and then use a local operator expansion trying to estimate the first-order corrections. Schematically, this can be written as follows:

$$\sum_n \mathcal{L}_{eff}^{(n)} = \mathcal{L}^{(0)} + \mathcal{L}^{(1)} + \mathcal{L}^{(2)} + \ldots, \tag{4.24}$$

where $\mathcal{L}^{(0)}$ represents the standard model, $\mathcal{L}^{(1)}$ is the first-order correction, and $\mathcal{L}^{(2)}$ is second-order correction. The idea then is to try to calculate the first- and second-order corrections by assuming that there will not be any Lorentz or gauge symmetry breaking terms (i.e. one assumes that $\mathcal{L}^{(i)}$ is $SU(3) \times SU(2) \times U(1)$ invariant and Lorentz invariant) and by increasing the value of the cutoff Λ in each correction term (for details see Georgi, 1991). Other examples of "bottom-up" approaches include the Fermi theory of low-energy weak interactions and chiral Lagrangians (Bain, 2013a; Georgi, 1993; Manohar and Wise, 2007).

In the "top-down" approach, on the other hand, one constructs a large length scale (low-energy scale) theory from a short length scale (high-energy scale) theory. The RG explanation of critical phenomena can be interpreted as a prime example of the "top-down" approach. Another example is the quantum Hall effect, which has also been considered a paradigmatic example of emergent behavior. Since we have already explained the theory of critical phenomena, let us now turn to the second example. The quantum Hall effect results from the application of a magnetic field to a group of electrons and has properties that are substantially different from the properties of the underlying electrons, such as incompressibility and dissipationless transport. More specifically, the high-energy theory of the quantum Hall liquid describes electrons moving in a two-dimensional conductor and coupled to an external magnetic field and to so-called Chern–Simons fields. This situation is described by the following nonrelativistic Lagrangian density:

$$\mathcal{L} = i\psi^{\dagger}\{\partial_t - ie(A_0 - a_0)\}\psi - (\frac{1}{2}m)\psi^{\dagger}\{\partial_i + ie(A_i + a_i)\}^2\psi + \mu\psi^{\dagger}\psi + \vartheta\epsilon^{\mu\nu\lambda}a_\mu\partial_\nu a_\lambda, \tag{4.25}$$

where ψ is the field variable that encodes the electron degrees of freedom, the pair (A_0, A_i) represents the degrees of freedom of an external magnetic field, $a_\mu (\mu = 1, 2, 3)$ represents the degrees of freedom of a Cherm–Simons field, μ is the chemical potential, and the coefficient ϑ is chosen in such a way that the electrons are coupled to an even number of internal magnetic fluxes (Bain, 2013a). If v, called the "filling factor," is an integer, the effect that arises in this interaction is called the Integer Quantum Hall Effect (IQHE). If v is given by simple fractions, more intriguing physics appears and there will be a formation of states that supports fractional excitations with particles having fractional statistics and even fractional electric charge. This is called the Fractional Quantum Hall Effect (FQHE).[26]

The properties of the quantum Hall liquid (e.g. incompressibility and dissipationless transport) can be derived from the high-energy theory (47) by integrating out the electron degrees of freedom (Bain, 2013a):

$$\mathcal{L}_{eff} = \vartheta \epsilon^{\mu\nu\lambda} a_\mu \partial_\nu a_\lambda + \vartheta' \epsilon^{\mu\nu\lambda} (A_\mu + a_\mu) \partial_\nu (A_\lambda + a\lambda), \tag{4.26}$$

where the coefficient ϑ' is chosen to produce the IQHE for the second Chern–Simons field. It is important to point out that this effective field theory is topologically distinct from the high-energy theory and the transition from one to the other cannot be described by a broken symmetry (in contrast to the transition from paramagnetism to ferromagnetism discussed in Section 2.4). In fact, the effective field theory $\mathcal{L}_{eff}$ describes a topological quantum field theory, in which a spacetime metric does not explicitly appear in the Lagrangian density (Bain, 2013a). We will see below that this formal difference between the effective and high-energy theory plays an important role in the discussion on emergence in EFTs.

In practice, in the "top-down" approach, arriving at a lower-energy theory (e.g. coarse-grained theory) from the high-energy theory (e.g. fine-grained theory) is not always a simple task, and external guidance such as experimental results are needed in order to find an adequate transformation that keeps the free energy and the relevant physics approximately invariant. So, *in practice*, the construction of the low-energy theory from the high-energy theory is not just a matter of *deducing* the former from the latter. Instead, usually a phenomenological investigation of the system is required in order to assure that the transformation will maintain the relevant physics (Bain, 2013b; Crowther, 2015; Luu and Meißner, 2019). Like the Wilsonian approach, in general, there is no "standard recipe" to construct EFTs (Kadanoff et al., 1976; Nienhuis et al., 1980).

This "lack of deducibility" has played an important role in the discussion on the emergence in ETFs. For instance, Cao and Schweber (1993) take this as a motivation for defending a pluralistic and antireductionist picture of the world, in which the world is supposed to be arranged into an infinite hierarchy of autonomous domains, each level having its own ontology and its own fundamental laws.[27] This antireductionist picture, which we can also interpret in terms of *strong emergence*, relies, on the one hand, on the idea

---

[26] See Shech (2015) and Bain (2016) for philosophical discussion on the emergence of the FQHE.
[27] A similar antirreductionist view has been recently defended by Ellis (2020).

that the low-energy theory cannot be simply derived from the high-energy theory without appealing to low-energy empirical information. On the other hand, it rests on "the decoupling theorem," which is a theorem that demonstrates that high-energy contributions have negligible effect on low-energy regimes.[28]

Bain (2013a, 2013b) developed a different antireductionist position. In contrast to Cao and Schweber, he does not defend strong emergence, and his argument does not rely on the decoupling theorem. Instead, he argues for the existence of *weak emergence* based on what he sees as a "substantial difference" between the low-energy and high-energy theories. More precisely, by analyzing examples of EFTs such as the quantum Hall effect mentioned above, he noticed that the Lagrangian (or Hamiltonian) density $\mathcal{L}_{eff}$ of the low-energy theory is formally distinct from the Lagrangian density $\mathcal{L}$ of the high-energy theory, which means that the former is a functional of effective field variables that do not appear in $\mathcal{L}$.[29] He points out that this is particularly clear in cases in which the degrees of freedom of the low-energy theory cannot be straightforwardly interpreted as coarse-grained degrees of freedom of the higher energy theory such as in the case of quantum chromodynamics (QCD). In fact, in QCD, a theory of strong interactions, the relevant degrees of freedom are quarks and gluons, whereas the low-energy description is given in terms of protons, neutrons and pions. Bain (2013a, 2013b) then associates this "substantial difference" between the low-energy and high-energy theories to the "lack of deducibility" of the former from latter and uses this as an an argument against the reduction of EFTs and as a basis to construct a notion of emergence in EFT. We can interpret this notion of emergence as *weak* and *ontological*. *Weak* because it is compatible with microphysicalism[30] and *ontological*, because the behavior described by the EFTs is assumed to be ontologically different from the behavior described by the high-energy theory.

Although many authors are sympathetic to the idea that EFTs describe emergent behavior (e.g. Butterfield, 2014; Crowther, 2015; Luu and Meißner, 2019), they do not all agree that emergence should be framed here in terms of "lack of deducibility," "lack of derivability," or even "failure of reduction."

---

[28] Hartmann (2001) criticizes this line of reasoning by pointing out that the decoupling theorem is valid only under restrictive conditions, for instance it requires the high-energy theory to be perturbatively renormalizable (see Rivat and Grinbaum, (2020) for a discussion around this debate).

[29] A Lagrangian density of a field theory $\mathcal{L}[\phi_i, \delta_\mu \phi_i]$, $i = 1 \ldots N$, $\mu = 0, 1, 2, 3$, is a functional of N field variables $\phi_i(x)$ and their first derivatives.

[30] He believes that microphysicalism is secured by the fact that the high-energy degrees of freedom are identified and integrated out of the Lagrangian $\mathcal{L}$.

For instance, Castellani (2002) and Hartmann (2001) point out that although extremely difficult *in practice*, it is sometimes possible *in principle* to derive quantitative results in EFT from the high-energy theory, for example, by solving high-energy models exactly or by the use of adequate approximation methods. Other philosophers, most notably Butterfield (2014) and Crowther (2015), have also stressed the importance of disentangling the notion of emergence from the notion of reduction in the context of EFT. An important reason for this is that there can be emergence (understood as *novelty*) of the low-energy theory with respect to the high-energy theory, even if the former could be *derived* in principle from the latter with an adequate transformation. Indeed, the fact that the low-energy theory can be in principle derived from a high-energy theory by means of a well-defined transformation does not preclude that the former has terms that do not appear in the high-energy theory. Let us illustrate this idea by hand of a simple example. In real-space renormalization, one can derive a coarse-grained description of the Ising model by successively coarse-graining the degrees of freedom of the fine-grained descriptions following the simple "majority rule" (Section 4.1.1). In this case, the "effective degrees of freedom" are no more than the average of the fine-grained degrees of freedom, but the coarse-grained description uses terms that are different from the original Hamiltonians. In fact, the effective Hamiltonians associated with coarse-grained descriptions are a function of different coupling constants and different degrees of freedom than the fine-grained Hamiltonians. Another example concerns QCD. In QCD, the relevant degrees of freedom are quarks and gluons. At lower energies, however, processes involving quarks and gluons "freeze out" and only hadronic degrees of freedom (i.e. protons, neutrons, pions) are available to the system, which are composite particles with no net color (i.e. charge). Although one cannot solve the equations in QCD at low energies, researchers have been developing a derivation of the hadron masses from QCD by using complicated numerical methods such as numerical Lattice Field calculations (Aoki et al., 2000; Asakawa et al., 2001; Lorcé, 2018). Nonetheless, even if this derivation would be possible, this would not imply that a description in terms of hadrons like nucleons (protons and neutrons) is not novel or useful to understand low-energy phenomena in nuclear physics, such as the formation of heavier elements like deuterium, helium, carbon and oxygen, or the appearance of giant dipole resonances (i.e. oscillatory behavior originated by the collective motion of large groups of nucleons). Luu and Meißner (2019) make a similar point and say:

> The examples of emergent phenomena above have little to no resemblance to their lower level constituents, which in this case are quarks and gluons. And since their description at the lower level via traditional calculations is

essentially all but impossible, physicists instead turn to the powerful tool of effective field theory, where instead of using the lower level constituents to frame the problem, they instead work directly with the emergent phenomena as the relevant degrees of freedom. (p. 3)

The aforementioned arguments suggest that lack of derivability is not necessary for the occurrence of novel properties and novel explanations in the EFT and therefore should not be at the basis of the concept of emergence in EFT. In Section 5, we will give further reasons to separate the concept of emergence from the concept of reduction.

Motivated by the decoupling of emergence and reduction, Crowther (2015) developed a conception of emergence in EFT that does not depend on the notion of derivability (neither in practice nor in principle). Instead of defining emergence in terms of "lack of derivability" or "failure of reduction," she gives a positive conception of emergence in terms of *novelty* and *autonomy*. By novelty, she means that the features of the low-energy description are not features of the high-energy description. In the case of EFTs, this comes from the fact that the low-energy theory is formally distinct from the high-energy theory (e.g. the degrees of freedom of the effective Lagrangian density are distinct from the degrees of freedom of the original Lagrangian density). By autonomy, she means that the low-energy theory is largely independent of the details of the high-energy theory. She calls this independence upon microscopic details "underdetermination" of the high-energy theory by the low-energy theory, but this can also be understood in terms of *robustness* defined in Section 4.2. Apart from robustness, she associates autonomy with *universality*, which is for her a stronger sense of autonomy in which several different high-energy systems give rise to the same low-level behavior.

Note that the notion of emergence developed by Crowther is largely compatible with the definition of "coarse-grained emergence" that I developed in Section 4.3. There are, however, small differences between Crowther's conception of emergence and the one that I suggested. First of all, she defines novelty only in terms of conceptual novelty, whereas I also emphasize the explanatory novelty of EFTs with respect to high-energy theories. Second, the definition that I suggest applies only to cases in which there are coarse-graining operations involved, whereas Crowther's definition does not seem to have such a restriction. In this sense, Crowther's definition can be thought of as more general than the one that I suggested. However, I believe that the definition offered in Section 4.3, by being more informative, gives us a richer understanding of a specific class of EFTs, in which the low-energy EFT is obtained by coarse-graining or by integrating out the degrees of freedom of the high-energy theory.

If we consider the distinctions made in Section 1.1, we can say that the notion of emergence in EFT that I am defending here is *weak* in the sense that it does not challenge microphysicalism (see Section 4.5), *epistemological*, in the sense that novelty is defined in epistemological terms such as conceptual difference and explanatory irreducibility,[31] and *synchronic*, because one compares different levels of descriptions of coexistent behavior.

Very recently, Luu and Meißner(2019) defended a similar notion of emergence for EFTs that can also be interpreted as *weak* and *epistemological*. More specifically, they understand emergence in terms of *conceptual novelty* (i.e. epistemological emergence) and *dependence* of the lower energy theory upon the high-energy degrees of freedom and the symmetries of the high-energy description (i.e. weak emergence). Interestingly, for them this notion of (weak) emergence is entirely compatible with reduction. In Section 5, I will come back to this discussion and I will give more arguments for the compatibility of emergence and (intertheoretic) reduction.

4.5 Remarks on the "Reductive" Character of the RG Approach

We have seen in this section that the use of the RG approach does not consist in a detailed microscopic description of the low-energy (or large length scale) behavior. To the contrary, one defines a RG transformation that subsequently coarse-grains the effective degrees of freedom and makes us "forget" about the irrelevant microscopic details underlying a particular behavior. However, it is important to bear in mind that the RG approach is not a phenomenological theory and it does appeal indirectly to the microscopic degrees of freedom of the original Hamiltonians (or Lagrangians), such as Ising spins. In fact, by coarse-graining or integrating out the degrees of freedom of the original Hamiltonians, the RG method establishes a (minimal) dependence of the lower-energy behavior upon the original microscopic degrees of freedom. This "dependency," as we argued in Section 4.3, can be understood in terms of the supervenience of the lower-energy behavior upon the microscopic degrees of freedom present in the original microscopic (high energy) description and serves to secure

---

[31] This does not rule out the possibility of interpreting emergence in some cases of EFTs in an ontological sense. However, in this context, affirming that emergence is not only epistemological but also ontological would require a further analysis of the relationship between specific EFTs and the world. This would involve metaphysical discussions, including discussions on the ontological status of the cutoff in RG methods. Such an analysis goes beyond the scope of this Element (for discussions on related issues see, for instance, Bain 2013a; Fraser, 2020; Georgi, 1993; Hartmann 2001; Huggett and Weingard, 1995; Rivat and Grinbaum, 2020; Williams, 2019).

microphysicalism. This is the reason why coarse-grained emergence, associated with the RG approach, should be interpreted as "weak" rather than "strong."

More generally, supervenience holds every time that there is a procedure that establishes the same type of dependence of the effective degrees of freedom on the dynamics of its constituent parts, as in the case of the EFT built from QCD mentioned above. As Luu and Meißner (2019) say:

> The interactions between nucleons are not disconnected from the interactions of quarks and gluons, however. They are related to their constituent parts in a rigorous, systematic manner. This procedure of relating the effective degrees of freedom to the dynamics of constituent parts collectively falls under the purview of effective field theory. We discuss tersely that within the EFT prescription, it is the symmetries of the lower level that dictates the allowed interaction terms at the higher level, but not the other way around. (p. 7)

Kadanoff (2013) makes a similar point for the case of critical phenomena:

> [T]he fixed-point concept describes a connection between the microscopic properties of the material, i.e. the interactions among its constituent particles and fields, and the behavior of the material on a conceptually infinite length scale. This connection is surprising and quite beautiful. (p. 35)

This "reductive" aspect of EFT in which one minimally establishes a dependence of the lower-energy behavior upon the degrees of freedom of the higher-energy description should not be forgotten. In fact, this aspect successfully establishes a connection between the different levels of description involved in the RG approach and assures that the effective or coarse-grained theory does not completely "float free" of the physical level described by the fine-grained theory. This is why some authors have considered the EFT framework as "intrinsically reductionist." Castellani (2002), for instance, argues:

> The EFT approach does not imply antireductionism, if antireductionism is grounded on the fact of emergence, as in the case of Anderson (1972) or Mayr (1988). The EFT schema, by allowing definite connections between the theory levels, provides an argument against the basic antireductionist claim of the scientists' debate. A reconstruction (the way up) is not excluded, even though it may have to be only in principle. (p. 265)

In some cases, such as the occurrence of critical behavior in the Ising model, we are confident that the behavior ultimately depends upon the degrees of freedom of the original model, and RG methods are used mainly with the purpose of explaining universal behavior or of predicting the critical exponents, especially when the partition function cannot be calculated exactly. However, there are cases in which the EFT approach is used principally with the purpose of establishing even a minimal dependence between the lower-energy behavior and the constituents of the high-energy description. The construction of EFTs on the basis of QCD may be an example of this.

4.6 Concluding Remarks

In this section, we have explained the main aspects of the RG approach by focusing on the explanation of universality and critical phenomena. We have also developed a concept of emergence that we called "coarse-grained emergence," which is different from the concept of "few-many emergence" developed in Section 3. We have argued that this concept fits particularly well with the case of critical phenomena and with an important class of EFTs. I finally emphasized some "reductive" aspects of the RG approach, which suggest that the notion of emergence associated with this class of EFTs should be interpreted as "weak" rather than "strong."

In the next section, I will examine in detail another reductive aspect of the RG approach that has to do with the use of limits in the construction of the coarse-grained theory from the fine-grained theory. This will serve to challenge the claim that the use of so-called "singular limits" imply a failure of reduction. At the same time, this will also serve to illustrate one of the main morals of this Element, namely that reduction is compatible with emergence.

5 Intertheoretic Reduction

In contrast to "few-many reduction" (Section 3), which describes a relationship between the properties of large aggregates and the properties of small systems, and to "coarse-grained emergence" (Section 4), which refers to the autonomy and novelty of coarse-grained descriptions with respect to fine-grained descriptions, "intertheoretic reduction" (as opposed to "intertheoretic emergence") describes more generally a relationship between theories. In the discussion around phase transitions and other cooperative phenomena, the failure of few-many reduction is widely accepted (e.g. Anderson, 1972; Butterfield, 2011b; Kadanoff, 2009; Norton, 2014), the existence of "coarse-grained emergence" is often recognized (Batterman, 2001, 2005; Crowther, 2015; Morrison, 2012), but the acceptance of intertheoretic reduction is still contentious. One of the reasons for this controversy has to do with the use of "singular limits" in the derivation of a phenomenological theory of phase transitions from a microscopic theory. For some (e.g. Batterman, 2001, 2005, 2011; Berry, 2002; Rueger, 2000), the appeal to singular limits implies the failure of intertheoretic reduction. For others (e.g. Ardourel, 2018; Butterfield, 2011a, 2011b; Norton, 2012, 2014; Palacios, 2019; Wayne, 2012), singular limits can be explained away in favor of reduction. In this section, I will give an overview of this discussion by focusing not only on the case of phase transitions, but also on other cases of singular limits, such as the van der Pol nonlinear oscillator (Rueger, 2000; Wayne, 2012). I will take the side of the reductionists by adding some remarks on the notion of intertheoretic reduction and by defending a compatibility between reduction and emergence.

5.1 Models of Intertheoretic Reduction

Very often, especially in the discussion around phase transitions, intertheoretic reduction is equated with the Nagelian model of reduction (or revised versions of it), in which reduction is understood in terms of *logical deduction*. However, it is important to bear in mind that philosophers of science present us with a number of models of reduction that should be taken into account when dealing with specific cases of intertheoretic reduction in physics, including the reduction of phase transitions. I will now explain some of these models, focusing on the ones that are more relevant for the case studies that we are concerned with in this Element[32].

Perhaps the most influential model of intertheoretic reduction is the Nagelian model, which Nagel introduced in 1949 and developed further in his celebrated 1961 book *The Structure of Science*. According to this model, a theory T_2, also called the "reduced theory" (e.g. the phenomenological theory, the high-level theory, the older theory or the secondary theory),[33] reduces to another theory T_1, called the "reducing theory" (e.g. the microscopic theory, the low-level theory, the new theory or the fundamental theory), if the laws of T_2 are *deducible* from the laws of T_1, under some auxiliary assumptions and sometimes with the help of *bridge laws* that connect the terms of T_1 and T_2. If the relevant terms in both theories are the same, bridge laws are not required and one has a case of *homogeneous reduction*. In cases of *inhomogeneous reduction*, at least one descriptive term in the reduced theory does not occur in the reducing theory, and bridge laws are required to connect the vocabulary of the reduced theory

---

[32] See Rosaler (2019) and Sklar (1967) for a discussion of different models of reduction.

[33] Note that "high-level theory" means here the macroscopic or phenomenological theory. This contrasts with the discussion on EFTs, in which "high-level theories" usually denote high-energy theories.

with the vocabulary of the reducing theory. In its most strict version, the model requires the reduced theory T_2 to be a logical consequence of T_1 plus bridge laws. A general formulation of this model is the following:

> **Nagelian reduction:** T_2 *reduces*$_{Nag}$ to T_1 iff the laws of T_2 can be logically deduced from the laws of T_1 along with bridge laws that connect the terms of T_1 and T_2.

In 1970, Nagel suggested a revision of this model that allows the reduced theory to be *approximately deduced* from the reducing theory.

Inspired by cases in which the theory that can be deduced from the reducing theory is not the original theory to be reduced, but a corrected version of it, Schaffner (1967) introduced the following model of reduction:[34]

> **Schaffner's reduction**: T_2 *reduces*$_{Sch}$ to T_1 iff there is a corrected version T_2^* of T_2 such that (i) the laws of T_2^* can be logically deduced from the laws of T_1 along with bridge laws and (ii) T_2 and T_2^* are *strongly analogous*.

Although there is no general characterization of "strong analogy," in most cases this signifies that the two theories are in close agreement or approximately equal, for example, with respect to the predictions that they make. Whether or not there is an approximation between T_2 and T_2^* depends on empirical considerations and is decided within the specific scientific discipline (Dizadji-Bahmani et al., 2010; Rosaler, 2019).

An important example of Schaffner's reduction, presented as a paradigmatic example of reduction by Schaffner himself, is the reduction of physical optics to Maxwell's electromagnetic theory.[35] In order to achieve the reduction of physical optics T_2 to the electromagnetic theory T_1, Sommerfeld modified the laws of physical optics T_2. In particular, on the basis of Maxwell's equations, he modified Fresnel's famous sine and tangent laws of the ratio of the relevant amplitudes of incident, reflected, and refracted polarized light. In other words, he constructed a modified version T_2^* of the original secondary theory T_2, which was approximately derived from a low-level theory T_1, which in this case corresponds to Maxwell's electromagnetic theory. This modified version of Fresnel's laws can be regarded as a close analogy of the original laws of physical optics, in the sense that it produces predictions that are very close to the predictions of physical optics. Dizadji-Bahmani et al. (2010) take the reduction

---

[34] This model has been called the "Generalized Nagel Schaffner model" by Dizadji-Bahmani et al. (2010)

[35] See Schaffner (1967) and Worrall (1989) for a detailed analysis of this reduction.

of the Second Law of Thermodynamics to statistical mechanics to be another instance of Schaffner's reduction.[36]

In his celebrated "Two Concepts of Intertheoretic Reduction," Nickles (1973) distinguishes yet another type of reduction, which he dubbed as *reduction₂* to differentiate it from what he called *reduction₁*, which corresponds to the Nagelian model. *Reduction₂*, or what we will call here "Nickles' reduction," consists in the recovery of one theory from another by invoking limiting operations or other appropriate transformations. In contrast to Nagelian reduction, Nickles' reduction is not restricted to a single logical relation but can involve a series of intertheoretic operations. More importantly, in Nickles reduction, the derivation of a theory from another should be understood in a broad sense, including limiting operations and approximations of many kinds.

Nickles (1973)'s reduction can be characterized as follows:

> **Nickles reduction:** Let O_i be a set of intertheoretic operations, then a theory T_2 *reduces*$_{Nick}$ to another T_1 iff $O_i(T_1) \rightarrow T_2$ and the operations O_i make physical sense.

Here the arrow represents "mathematical derivation" understood in a broad sense.[37] Roughly, this schema means that by performing a set of mathematical operations O_i on T_1, one obtains T_2.

Now, as Palacios (2019) points out, one should note that mathematical operations such as limits and other approximations are performed not on the theory itself but on functions (or equations) representing physical quantities. Thus a more precise schema of Nickles' reduction needs to be formulated in terms of the functions (quantities) that play a relevant role in the reduction rather than in terms of the theories to be compared. Given these considerations, Palacios offers the following revised formulation of Nickles' reduction:

> **Nickles reduction*:** Given a set of intertheoretic operations O_i, a quantity Q^1 of T_1 *reduces*$_{Nick^*}$ a quantity Q^2 of T_2, iff (i) $O_i(Q^1) \rightarrow Q^2$ and (ii) the mathematical operations O_i make physical sense.

Although Nickles is not explicit about what he means by "physical sense," one can interpret this constraint as signifying that after applying a set of

---

[36] See Callender (1999); Dizadji-Bahmani et al. (2010), Robertson (2020); Sklar (1999); Uffink (2001) for a philosophical discussion around the reduction of the Second Law. Unfortunately, lack of space prevents me from reviewing this discussion.

[37] For Nickles, in *reduction₂*, one says that the macroscopic theory reduces to the microscopic theory under certain mathematical operations. This inversion in the direction of the reduction is motivated by the way in which physicists talk about reduction. Since this is not important to understand this approach to reduction, I will stick to the philosophers' jargon.

mathematical operations on T_1, the resulting theory can still describe realistic behavior. Taking the limit of a constant of nature to zero, for example, may result in a theory that does not account for realistic behavior, unless this limit is adequately explained. Similarly, taking the limit of a parameter such as the number of particles to infinity may also be illegitimate if this limit is not adequately justified.[38]

A special case of Nickles' reduction is "limiting reduction," which refers to cases in which the transformations consist in mathematical limits. In cases where one limit is used, one can characterize *limiting reduction* as follows:

> **Limiting reduction:** Let Q^1 denote a relevant quantity of T_1, Q^2 a relevant quantity of T_2, then a quantity Q^2 of T^2 *reduces$_{lim}$* to a corresponding quantity Q^1 of T_1 iff (ii) $\lim_{N\to\infty} Q_N^1 = Q^2$ or $\lim_{N\to0} Q_N^1 = Q^2$ (where N represents a parameter appearing in T_1) and (ii) the limiting operation makes physical sense.

Condition (i) means that the values of the physical quantity Q^1 of T_1 should converge in the limit $N \to \infty$ (or $N \to 0$) to the values of the physical quantity Q^2 of T_2.[39]

Batterman (2001, p. 19) represents condition (i) of *limiting reduction* by the following schema:

$$\lim_{\epsilon \to 0} T_1 = T_2, \tag{5.1}$$

where ϵ is a small expansion or perturbation parameter. He points out that this schema is satisfied in cases of *regular* limits, which he describes as cases in which "the exact solutions for small but nonzero values of $|\epsilon|$ smoothly approach the unperturbed or zeroth-order solution [ϵ set identically equal to zero] as $\epsilon \to 0$" (Batterman 2001, p. 79). A case considered to be a paradigmatic example of limiting reduction (Batterman, 2001; Nickles, 1973; Rueger, 2000) is the reduction of Einsteinian formula for momentum:

$$p_1 = \frac{m_0 v}{\sqrt{1 - \frac{v^2}{c^2}}}, \tag{5.2}$$

---

[38] See Rosaler (2019) and Palacios (2018) for a discussion on the justification of infinite limits.

[39] This convergence can be either uniform or pointwise. However, since uniform convergence is stronger than pointwise convergence, if the values of the quantities converge uniformly, the limiting reduction will be stronger than if they only converge pointwise. For this reason some authors (e.g. Rueger, 2000, 2004) have decided to restrict limiting reduction to cases of uniform convergence (see Palacios and Valente (2021) for a discussion on these two types of convergence in the context of limiting reduction.)

to the corresponding formula in classical mechanics $p_2 = m_0 v$ in the limit $(c/v)^2 \to 0$. This is an example of a regular limit because the expression $\sqrt{1 - \frac{v^2}{c^2}}$ can be expanded in a Taylor series as:

$$1 - 1/2(v/c)^2 - 1/8(v/c)^4 - 1/16(v/c)^6 - \ldots \tag{5.3}$$

This means that momentum in special relativity can be written in terms of momentum in classical mechanics plus an expansion in powers of $(v/c)^2$ (Batterman 2001; Rueger 2000).

Condition (ii) of limiting reduction can be interpreted again as signifying that after applying a mathematical limit on T_1, the resulting theory can still describe realistic behavior. Butterfield (2011b) suggested a criterion for the justification of infinite limits that Landsman (2013) called "Butterfield Principle," which says that a limit is justified as being mathematically convenient and empirically adequate if the values of the quantities evaluated in the limit at least approximate the values of the quantities "on the way to the limit," that is, for large but finite values N_0 of the parameter N, that is, if $Q_\infty \approx Q_{N_0}$[40] and if the behavior "on the way to the limit" is the one that is physically real.

5.2 The Problem of Singular Limits

Batterman (1995, 2001, 2005, 2019) and Rueger (2000, 2004), among others, have argued that limiting reduction, and more generally, intertheoretic reduction, fails in cases of "singular limits," and they associate this failure of intertheoretic reduction to the existence of emergent behavior. More precisely, in *Devil in the Details*, Batterman (2001) defines emergent behavior as "a result of the singular nature of the limiting relationship between the finer and coarser theories that are relevant to the phenomenon of interest" (p. 121) and he interprets this notion of emergence in an ontological sense, suggesting that the singular behavior captured by a singular limit denotes real behavior, which is ontologically distinct from the behavior that appears in finite systems. Later (Batterman 2011), he seems to move toward an epistemological conception, in which emergence is understood as an epistemic failure, meaning that certain concepts of the phenomenological theory cannot be predicted or explained in terms of the microscopic theory.

In order to better understand Rueger's and Batterman's conception of emergence, one needs to understand the notion of "singular limits." He defines

---

[40] More precisely, if $|Q_{N=\infty} - Q_{N_0}| < \epsilon$, where ϵ is taken to be small and N_0 represents a realistic value (see also Palacios, 2018).

singular limits as cases in which the "behavior in the limit is of a *fundamentally different character* than the nearby solutions one obtains as $\epsilon \to 0$" (Batterman 2001, p. 19). In other words, these are cases in which schema (5.1) fails, namely:

$$\lim_{\epsilon \to 0} T_1 \neq T_2.$$

In our terminology, these are cases in which the values of the quantities as $N \to \infty$ do not converge to the quantities evaluated in the limit $N = \infty$:

$$\lim_{N \to \infty} Q_N^1 \neq Q_{N=\infty}^2$$

In other words, singular limits represent cases in which condition (i) of limiting reduction fails.

Apart from the case of phase transitions that we will discuss in Sections 5.3 and 5.4, an example that has been extensively analyzed in the debate on singular limits is the van der Pol oscillator (e.g. Rueger, 2000, 2004; Wayne, 2012). The van der Pol oscillator is a nonconservative oscillator with nonlinear damping. Experimenting with this system shows that its short timescale behavior is very different from its long-term behavior. In fact, for any short timescale, the system's behavior is close to a simple harmonic oscillator, whereas for a long timescale, its behavior is dominated by the rate of change of amplitude and, independently of the initial value of the amplitude, the oscillations have a "limit cycle," which means that the system tends toward a unique periodic behavior. Given this difference between the short-term and long-term behavior, two different theories are used to describe the behavior in each case. Short-timescale behavior is modeled as a simple harmonic oscillator, whereas long-timescale behavior is described by using a linear model of the change of amplitude over time and ignoring the harmonic motion entirely. The question that arises is how these two theories are related, and, more precisely, whether the theory that describes the long-term behavior can be reduced to the theory describing the short time-scale behavior.

Let us examine this example in some detail. The amplitude of oscillations, $x(t)$ in the van der Pol oscillator is given by the following equation:

$$x'' - \eta(1 - x^2)x' + x = 0, \tag{5.4}$$

where $x' = dx/dt$ and η is a parameter that measures the strength of the damping term $-(1 - x^2)x'$. For $\eta = 0$, Eq. (5.4) reduces to the equation for a simple harmonic oscillator, which describes the behavior of the system for short-time scales. One would then expect to describe the situation for small damping by adding small corrections to the expression for the simple harmonic oscillator.

In other words, one would expect that the general solution can be written as an expansion around $\eta = 0$ in the form:

$$x(t) = x_{\eta=0}(t) + \eta\xi_1(t) + \eta^2\xi_2(t) + \ldots, \tag{5.5}$$

and for all values of the independent variable t. However, over a long timescale, the expansion (5.5) "breaks down," which means that the solutions for $\eta = 0$ will be radically different from the solutions for $0 < \eta << 1$. In fact, for large enough t, we arrive at an expansion for the amplitude of the form:

$$x(t) = \cos\omega t + k\eta(t\cos\omega t) + \ldots, \tag{5.6}$$

where k is a constant, the first term corresponds to the solution of the undamped harmonic oscillator with frequency ω, but the second term is unbounded for $t \to \infty$. The appearance of such a second term is due to the nonlinearity of the system. A consequence of this is that for large enough t, the values of the Eq. (5.6) as $\eta \to 0$ do not converge uniformly to the values of the equation evaluated in the limit $\eta = 0$, that is:

$$\lim_{\eta \to 0} Q^1 \neq Q^2_{\eta=0}.$$

The limit $\eta \to 0$ is then said to be a singular limit.

Rueger (2000) concludes from this that there is a failure of inter-theoretic reduction. In fact, he argues that a consequence of this is that the theory of the lightly damped van der Pol oscillator cannot be reduced to the theory of the undamped case, for $\eta = 0$. Moreover, he argues that this implies that there are emergent properties in the theory of the lightly damped van der Pol oscillator that cannot be captured by the theory of the undamped oscillators, such as the limit cycle properties mentioned above.[41]

Although plausible, Rueger's approach has been target of considerable criticism. Wayne (2012), for instance, has argued against Rueger's view, by showing that the behavior of the van der Pol oscillator over a long timescale can be derived to an arbitrary degree of accuracy from the theory describing its short-term behavior by using singular perturbation techniques. In particular, he shows that if one assumes that the amplitude and phase of the solution vary slowly with respect to the period of oscillation, the Krylov–Bogoliubov–Mitropolsky (KBM) method, allows for the following expansion:

$$x = a\cos\psi + \epsilon u_1(a,\psi) + \epsilon^2 u_2(a,\psi) + \ldots, \tag{5.7}$$

---

[41] Batterman (2001) arrives at a similar conclusion for the case of phase transitions. This argument will be examined in the Section 5.3.

where the u_i terms are periodic functions of ψ with period 2π, a is the amplitude of the first fundamental harmonic as a function of time, and ψ is the frequency of the first fundamental harmonic as a function of time. This expression is limited to a finite number of terms and in the case of the van der Pol oscillator it is enough to consider terms up to ϵ^2 to infer the long-term behavior, which is mathematically treatable. Moreover, the KBM method to the order of ϵ^2 can be used to derive the limit cycle properties that characterize long-term behavior.

Now, as Wayne (2012) himself notices, this method requires additional empirical information that goes beyond the basic equation of motion of the van der Pol oscillator and the initial conditions. In fact, one needs to assume that amplitude and phase do not vary quickly relative to the period of oscillation. This means that in this case one does not derive the theory of long-term behavior from the equation that describes short-term behavior alone. However, Wayne (2012) points out that the assumption that is needed to connect the two theories can be expressed exclusively in terms of the theory of short term behavior, such as harmonic oscillation, amplitude, and phase. There is, therefore, no need to refer to *concepts* of the theory of long-term behavior. This is why Wayne (2012) concludes that the theory of long-term behavior is reducible to the theory of short-term behavior in spite of the presence of singular limits. In fact, the KBM method helps one approximately derive the theory of long-term behavior from the short-term behavior of the van der Pol oscillator plus certain phenomenological assumptions. In this sense, it satisfies the two conditions of Nickles' reduction, which, as we saw, are not restricted to limiting operations.

A possible objection to this line of reasoning was pointed out by McGivern (2007). He argues that the KBM method requires a distinction between the two characteristic timescales in the behavior of the van der Pol oscillator. In fact, the explanation of the long-term behavior begins with the assumption that over a long timescale there is a change in amplitude. According to McGivern, the fact that we need to distinguish between short and long timescales blocks the reduction:

> In terms of the distinction between "levels" suggested by the perturbation techniques itself – the fast and slow timescales – basal explainability seems to fail since predicting the limit cycle behavior involves explicitly recognizing the different timescales characterizing the system. (McGivern, 2007, p. 7)

However, Wayne offers a compelling reply to this objection by pointing out that the distinction between scales is a consequence of a phenomenological investigation of the system, which is essential to give an inter-level explanation. He says: "If prior recognition of distinct levels vitiates basal explanation, as McGivern suggests, then no upper-level property is basally explainable" (Wayne, 2012, p. 350).

We will see next that in the case of phase transitions, a phenomenological investigation of the system is also needed in order to know what limits to take. We will conclude, in the same vein as Wayne, that this does not imply a failure of inter-theoretic reduction. Indeed, we will argue that the idea that we cannot assume any phenomenological assumption in the reduction of a theory to another theory is a consequence of a notion of reduction that is too strict to account for the most important cases of inter-theoretic reduction in physics. Moreover, I will argue in Section 5.7 that such a strong notion of reduction is not needed to achieve the main goals of reductive projects in the history of physics, and that a much weaker notion of reduction that admits approximations and phenomenological observations can suffice to achieve those goals.

5.3 Dissolving the Problem of Singular Limits for First-Order Phase Transitions

Let us now return to our prime example, namely phase transitions. In the discussion around a possible intertheoretic reduction of phase transitions, what has been at stake is whether the *thermodynamical treatment* of phase transitions, from now on *TD* (i.e. singularities or discontinuities in the derivatives of the free energy), reduces to the *statistical mechanical treatment* of the phenomena, henceforth *SM*. Since both first-order and continuous phase transitions appear to involve the use of "singular limits" (Sections 2 and 3), they both have been regarded as candidates for a failure of inter-theoretic reduction, and consequently for some sort of emergent behavior associated with a failure of this type of reduction.

The view that intertheoretic reduction fails in the case of first-order phase transitions has been most prominently developed by Batterman (2001, 2005, 2011). As mentioned in Section 3.3, for Batterman, the failure of intertheoretic reduction is a consequence of the need for the thermodynamic limit ($N, V \rightarrow \infty$) in the derivation of the discontinuities in the derivatives of the free energy that successfully describe phase transitions in thermodynamics (see also Section 2.1). According to Batterman, the thermodynamic limit is a singular limit, because no matter how large we take the number of particles N to be, as long as the system remains finite, the derivatives of the free energy will never display a discontinuity. This allegedly implies that schema (49), $\lim_{\epsilon \rightarrow 0} T_1 = T_2$, fails, since the behavior at the limit is said to be qualitatively different from the behavior "on the way to the limit," that is, for N large but finite.

The idea that we can find analytic partition functions that "approximate" singularities is mistaken, because the very notion of approximation required fails to make sense if the limit is singular. The behavior at the limit (the physical discontinuity, the phase transition) is qualitatively different from the behavior as that limit is approached. (Batterman, 2005, p. 236)

Note also that if this is the case, then condition (i) of limiting reduction also fails, that is,

$$\lim_{N \to \infty} Q_N^{SM} \neq Q^{SM\infty},$$

where Q_N^{SM} represents the values of the quantities in finite statistical mechanics as $N \to \infty$ and $Q^{SM\infty}$ represents the values of the quantities evaluated in infinite statistical mechanics, for which "$N = \infty$."

Although this position has been very influential in the philosophy of science literature, it has also been target of a number of criticisms (e.g. Ardourel, 2018; Menon and Callender, 2011; Norton, 2012; Palacios, 2019). Perhaps the most important criticism for the case of first order phase transitions was pointed out by Butterfield (2011b), who challenged Batterman's conclusion by arguing that if one focuses on the relevant quantities that explain the actual behavior of phase transitions, the problem of "singular limits" can be solved in favor of reduction. Butterfield illustrates this idea with the following toy example. Consider the following sequence of functions:

$$g_N(x) = \begin{cases} -1 & \text{if } x \leq -1/N \\ N_x & \text{if } -1/N \leq x \leq 1/N) \\ 1 & \text{if } x \geq 1/N \end{cases}.$$

As N goes to infinity, the sequence converges pointwise to the discontinuous function:

$$g_\infty(x) = \begin{cases} -1 & \text{if } x < 0 \\ 0 & \text{if } x = 0 \\ 1 & \text{if } x > 0 \end{cases}$$

One can also introduce another function f, such that:

$$f = \begin{cases} 1 & \text{if } g \text{ is continuous} \\ 0 & \text{if } g \text{ is discontinuous} \end{cases}$$

If one focuses on f, then one may conclude, in the same vein as Batterman, that the behavior of g_∞ at the limit "$N = \infty$" is *fundamentally different* from the behavior of g when N is arbitrarily large but finite, which means that limiting reduction fails. However, Butterfield notices that if we focus instead on the behavior of the function g_N, we will see that the limit value of the function is approached continuously. This means that the limit system is not "singular" in the previous sense and that condition (i) of limiting reduction holds, that is: $\lim_{N \to \infty} g_N = g_\infty$.

According to Butterfield, this is exactly what happens with classical phase transitions and, for the case of first-order phase transitions, he seems right.[42] Indeed, in a system containing a finite number of particles and confined to a restricted geometry, the thermodynamic quantities that describe first-order phase transitions such as density and magnetization are continuous and vary smoothly with the relevant parameters. However, if we introduce a quantity f representing the discontinuity of such quantities and attribute a value 1 to f if the quantity is discontinuous and 0 if it is not discontinuous (analogously to the function f in Butterfield's example), then we might conclude that such a quantity has values evaluated at the limit $N = \infty$ that are qualitatively different from the values of the of the quantities "on the way to the limit," that is, for finite but large N. However, if we focus on the behavior of the thermodynamic quantities *themselves*, namely density for the liquid–gas transition and magnetization for the change of magnetization of a ferromagnet at sub-critical temperatures, we will arrive at a different conclusion. In fact, as N grows, we will observe that the change in these thermodynamic quantities becomes steeper and steeper so that the quantities smoothly approach a discontinuity in the limit, which is analogous to function g in the toy example (see Section 3.3). More importantly, a theoretical analysis of those situations also shows that these limits make physical sense, since one can demonstrate that for realistic values of N, the gradient in the derivatives of the free energy F^{SM} is sufficiently steep so that the difference in the limit values of the thermodynamic quantities evaluated in the limit F^{SM}_∞ and the quantities in realistic systems with finite and realistic N_0 becomes negligibly small, that is: $|F^{SM}_\infty - F^{SM}_{N_0}| < \epsilon$ (Fisher and Berker, 1982; Kadanoff, 2009; Schmelzer and Ulbricht, 1987).

The important lesson from Butterfield's argument is that the "singular" nature of the thermodynamic limit does not imply that there are no models of statistical mechanics that approximate the thermodynamic behavior of phase transitions, for N sufficiently large but finite. For him, this should be taken as

---

[42] Even if Butterfield aims to make a more general claim, this solution does not apply to all cases of "singular limits." Landsman (2013), for instance, shows that for the case of quantum systems displaying SSB and the classical limit $\hbar \to 0$ of quantum mechanics, the situation is different and much more challenging (see also Schmelzer and Ulbricht, 1987; Wallace, 2018). It seems therefore that the analysis of singular limits and the way of "dissolving the mystery" around them should be done on a case-by-case basis.

supporting the claim that the discontinuities that describe phase transitions in the limit are not physically real, but rather that they approximate the behavior of realistic systems. For us, this should also be taken as an argument in favor of the existence of *limiting reduction* between *SM* and *SM*$^\infty$ for the case of first-order phase transitions.

One needs to be careful, however, in not concluding that the previous argument resolves all the controversy around the reduction of phase transitions. First of all, it is important to bear in mind that we have addressed only the case of classical phase transitions and that quantum phase transitions have not been considered. Second, one needs to note that we have not considered the use of RG methods yet, in which, as mentioned in Section 4, there are two important infinite limits involved. This is precisely the issue that we are going to address next.

5.4 Dissolving the Problem of Singular Limits for Continuous Phase Transitions

As was shown in Section 4, the inference of the thermodynamic behavior of continuous phase transitions requires the appeal to RG methods. Batterman (2017) has suggested that the use of RG methods poses a further challenge for the project of reducing phase transitions to finite statistical mechanics. He attributes this difficulty to (i) the need for abstract explanations, which was addressed in Section 4.3, and (ii) the use of the thermodynamic limit in the inference of nontrivial fixed point solutions, which is allegedly necessary for the computation of critical exponents and for giving an account of universality (see Section 4.1). Batterman (2017, 571) claims:

> Crucial, of course, to finding a fixed point, is the fact that at criticality the correlation length diverges. Unless one has correlations of infinite extent, the iterative blocking procedure will get hung up at a given length scale and one will not find the fixed point.

From this paragraph it is clear that Batterman associates the existence of a fixed point to the divergence of the correlation length, which implies taking the thermodynamic limit. However, what he overlooks is that in continuous phase transitions there is a second infinite limit involved, which corresponds to iterating infinitely many times the RG transformations (Section 4.1.4). In real-space renormalization, this second limit, which I call "infinite iteration limit," can be written as $K^* = \lim_{n \to \infty} R_b^n(K_c)$, where n corresponds to the number of iterations of the RG transformation and K_c is the set of coupling constants of the original Hamiltonian with infinite correlation length ξ (analogous to Eq. 4.6).

Palacios (2019) points out that realizing that there is a second limit is crucial because it allows us to see that the set of mathematical limits involved in the statistical mechanical treatment of continuous phase transitions is not singular in Batterman's sense. In fact, one can demonstrate that once the thermodynamic limit is taken ($N, V \rightarrow \infty$), the infinite iteration limit ($n \rightarrow \infty$) approaches smoothly the nontrivial fixed point solutions K^* that allow one to calculate the values of the critical exponents, so that the following expression holds: $\lim_{n \rightarrow \infty} \lim_{N \rightarrow \infty} K_{N,n} = K^*$. This is a consequence of the analyticity of the RG flow, which is a basic assumption of the RG framework (see Goldenfeld, 1992).

After recognizing the existence of two infinite limits, Palacios (2019) points out, that the problem of continuous phase transitions is not that the set of infinite limits is singular in Batterman's sense, but instead that these two limits do not commute. Indeed, taking the infinite iteration limit after the thermodynamic limits allows one to find nontrivial fixed-point solutions, but taking the infinite iteration limit before the thermodynamic limit (i.e., in systems with large but finite values of N) leads to trivial fixed points $K = 0, K = \infty$, which do not allow one to calculate the correct values of the critical exponents. In other words, this means that $\lim_{N \rightarrow \infty} \lim_{n \rightarrow \infty} K_{n,N} \neq K^*$, where K^* represents the set of coupling constants of the nontrivial fixed point. The reason for this result is that in every finite system there will be a characteristic length scale associated to the size of the system. Therefore, the application of a coarse-graining transformation beyond that length will no longer maintain physical properties of the system and the "RG flow" will inevitably move toward a trivial fixed point, with values of the coupling constants either $K = 0$ or $K = \infty$ (details in Goldenfeld, 1992).

Is this noncommutability of the limits compatible with the reduction of critical phase transitions? Palacios (2019) argues that it is. In fact, what the reductionist must realize is that the infinite iteration limit is needed *only* if we consider an infinite system in the first place, this means, only if we take the thermodynamic limit first. But if we consider a large but finite system, *there is no need* to take the infinite iteration limit in order to find solutions that approximate the nontrivial fixed-point solutions obtained by taking the two limits . Indeed, there are topological and numerical arguments suggesting the possibility of finding approximate nontrivial fixed-point solutions in finite systems, which are infinitesimally close to the solutions obtained by taking the two infinite limits (Palacios, 2019). Recently, Wu (2021) has offered more arguments in this direction. These arguments give us good reason to conclude that the behavior in the limits "$N = \infty$" and "$n = \infty$" can be approximated by the behavior "on the way to the limits" and, moreover, for realistic values of N and n. This means that condition (ii) of limiting reduction also holds for the case of continuous phase transitions and that the presence of "singular limits" does not challenge the intertheoretic reduction of the thermodynamic treatment to the statistical mechanical treatment amended by RG methods.

At this stage, it is important to emphasize that in order to obtain nontrivial fixed point solutions that can explain the behavior of critical phase transitions in both finite and infinite systems, one needs to construct RG transformations that leave the partition function approximately invariant. This usually requires a phenomenological investigation of the system, which helps us deciding which are the microscopic variables of least direct importance and which are of most importance for the macroscopic phenomenon under investigation (Fisher, 1998). At the same time, empirical considerations need to be taken into account in order to decide which limits to take and in what order. This reinforces Wayne's contention that a phenomenological investigation is usually required to achieve intertheoretic reductions.

5.5 Nagelian Reduction, Limiting Reduction, and Emergence Combined

We have seen in the previous sections that the presence of "singular limits" does not imply the failure of intertheoretic reduction. However, in discussing the reduction of phase transitions, we focused only on the reduction between finite statistical mechanics and infinite statistical mechanics, and we did not analyze the relationship between these theories and thermodynamics. In order to establish a connection between the quantities of statistical mechanics and thermodynamics, another reduction is needed, which involves the use of bridge laws that connect the relevant terms in infinite statistical mechanics and thermodynamics.

In the case of first-order phase transitions, one usually constructs a bridge law that relates the thermodynamic derivatives of the free energy F^{TD} with the corresponding quantities in infinite statistical mechanics F^{SM_∞}. Once this bridge law is defined, one can actually *deduce* the thermodynamic treatment of phase transitions from the statistical mechanical treatment in the limit "$N = \infty$" (Butterfield, 2011b). In other words, one uses Nagelian reduction to recover the exact thermodynamic theory of phase transitions from infinite statistical mechanics. This means that in conventional approaches to first-order phase transitions, the reduction of the thermodynamic treatment of phase transitions involves the following two main steps: (i) a limiting reduction between the quantities of finite statistical mechanics SM and infinite statistical mechanics SM_∞, and (ii) a Nagelian reduction between infinite statistical mechanics and the thermodynamic treatment of phase transitions (see Figure 9).

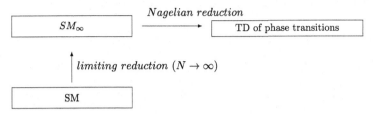

Figure 9 Schema for the reduction of first-order phase transitions

Analogously, in the case of continuous phase transitions, one needs bridge laws that connect the nontrivial fixed-point solutions with the values of critical exponents that characterize the phenomenological or thermodynamical behavior (Palacios, 2019). This is usually done after taking the thermodynamic limit $N \to \infty$ and the infinite iteration limit $n \to \infty$. In other words, the reduction of continuous phase transitions involves three main steps: (i) a limiting reduction that brings us to a system with infinite correlation length ξ, (ii) a limiting reduction that brings us to a coarse-grained system represented by a fixed-point K^*, and (iii) a Nagelian reduction that helps deriving the thermodynamic (phenomenological) behavior from the coarse-grained model (see Figure 10).

In addition, in the case of continuous phase transitions, this reduction is accompanied by the two notions of emergence discussed in Sections 3 and 4, namely "few-many emergence" and "coarse-grained emergence." There is few-many emergence because, as explained in Section 3.4, as the size of the system gets bigger ($N \to \infty$), fluctuations with different sizes start dominate the behavior with correlations that persist over distances comparable to the correlation length ξ, and this behavior cannot be observed in (or predicted by) very small systems. There is also coarse-grained emergence because, as we saw in Section 4.1, in order to cope with the problem of large correlation length in the case of continuous phase transitions, one successively coarse-grains the system ($n \to \infty$) until one reaches out information about parts of the system that are far away (see Section 4.1). The coarse-graining description allows one to predict the behavior close to the critical point and to explain universality, but involves terms that are novel with respect to fine-grained descriptions and it is also autonomous with respect to fine-grained descriptions in the sense of being robust and universal (Section 4.3).

Figure 10 illustrates the main steps in the reduction of the phenomenological treatment of critical phase transitions to statistical mechanics. Note that the notions of "few-many emergence" and "coarse-grained emergence" are partially captured here by the use of the limits $N \to \infty$ and $n \to \infty$, respectively, which we argued are reductive operations (in the sense of "limiting reduction").

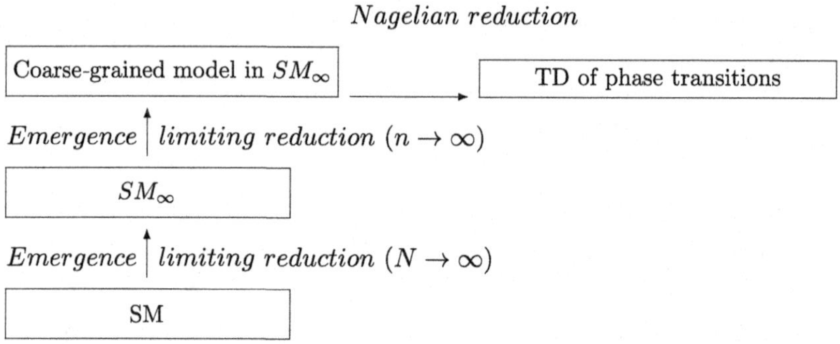

Nagelian reduction

| Coarse-grained model in SM_∞ | | TD of phase transitions |

$Emergence$ ↑ *limiting reduction* $(n \rightarrow \infty)$

| SM_∞ |

$Emergence$ ↑ *limiting reduction* $(N \rightarrow \infty)$

| SM |

Figure 10 Schema for the reduction of continuous phase transitions

This means that these notions of emergence are perfectly compatible with the reduction of the phenomenological theory of continuous phase transitions to microscopic theories.

It is important to emphasize that although the limits help "capturing" the emergent behavior that arises close to the critical point, they are not *needed* for the explanation or prediction of this behavior. In fact, we argued in Section 5.4 that the novel behavior that characterizes the "few-many emergence" in continuous phase transitions arises also "on the way to the limit," that is, for large but finite values of N (see also Butterfield, 2011b). We also argued that the novel behavior that characterizes "coarse-grained emergence" in continuous phase transitions arises "on the way to the limit" $n \rightarrow \infty$, i.e. for large but finite values of n (Palacios, 2019). This suggests, *pace* Batterman (2001, 2017), that, although pragmatically useful, the use of "singular limits" is not indispensable for the explanations of continuous phase transitions and does not imply a failure of intertheoretic reduction.

5.6 EFT, Intertheoretic Reduction, and Emergence

Let us now return to the discussion on EFTs initiated in Section 4.4. We said that an important class of EFTs is constructed by means of RG methods. In the Wilsonian approach, one constructs the lower-energy theory T_2 (or more precisely, a series of lower-energy theories) from the high-energy theory T_1 by letting the number of iterations n of the RG transformation go to infinity. For what has been said in the present section, this can be interpreted as a *limiting reduction* between T_1 and T_2 that coarse-grains the system indefinitely. This means that at least for a class of EFTs, emergence (as discussed in Section 4) is compatible with intertheoretic reduction. Furthermore, if we assume a more liberal notion of intertheoretic reduction (e.g. Nickles' reduction) that includes not only limiting relations, but also other approximation relations, such as saddle point approximation, a broader class of EFTs can be regarded as successful intertheoretic reductions.

Recently, many authors (e.g. Butterfield, 2011a, 2011b; Crowther, 2015; 2011b, Luu and Meißner, 2019, Rivat and Grinbaum, 2020) have defended the compatibility of emergence and reduction in the context of EFTs, but most of them still understand intertheoretic reduction in terms of Nagelian reduction. For instance, Rivat and Grinbaum (2020), who stress the role of approximations and empirical input in the construction of EFTs, say:

> [T]he relation between two EFTs involves approximations and heuristic reasoning: e.g. performing a saddle point approximation when integrating out heavy field or taking the zero mass limit of some light field... Here, again, successful Nagelian reductions are relatively permissive to the use of intermediary approximations, assumptions, and heuristic reasoning. The ultimate goal of a Nagelian reduction is to explain away the success of the low-energy theory by means of the high-energy theory, not to provide a strict derivation relying only on the resources of the high-energy theory. (p. 13)

Although it is true that the Nagelian model admits approximations (Butterfield, 2011a; Dizadji-Bahmani et al., 2010; Nagel, 1970), this model puts an emphasis on the logical deduction of a theory from another and the bridge laws connecting the terms in the theories to be compared. On the other hand, Nickles' model of reduction focuses on the approximation relations between theories and, in special cases, on the limiting relations between them. Based on this distinction, which was first suggested by Nickles (1973) himself, cases in which the reduction of a theory to another is achieved through approximation relations such as limiting operations should be rather interpreted as instances of Nickles' reduction, and more specifically limiting reduction. If the reduction also involves the use of bridge laws, then the case should be interpreted as a combination of Nickles' model of reduction and Nagelian reduction, such as in the example of phase transitions (Section 5.5).

It is also important to point out that intertheoretic reduction (understood as a combination of models) is perfectly compatible with assumptions coming from a phenomenological investigation of the system. In fact, we argued above that in cases of limiting reduction, one generally needs external input to decide which limits to take and in what order. Similarly, Nagelian reduction is also compatible with the use of auxiliary assumptions and bridge laws coming from an empirical investigation of the system (Butterfield, 2014). For what is more, Schaffner's reduction allows for a modification of the lower-energy (large length scale) theory on the basis of the high-energy (short length scale) theory. The crucial aspect of intertheoretic reduction, as Rivat and Grinbaum (2020) suggest, is that it should serve to fulfill certain goals. In fact, I will argue in Section 5.7 that this liberal notion of reduction, in which reduction is taken as a combination of models, is sufficient to achieve the most important goals of intertheoretic reduction and allows us to account for successful cases of reduction in physics, such as the reduction of the theory of critical phenomena and other EFTs.

5.7 Concluding Remarks: The Goals of Intertheoretic Reduction

In this section, we have reviewed the most important models of inter-theoretic reduction and have argued that they are compatible with emergence, as defined in Sections 3 and 4. Since the two concepts of emergence discussed here involve a notion of "novelty," this means that intertheoretic reduction is compatible with the existence of novel terms in the reduced or macroscopic theory, which are not present in the reducing or microscopic theory. As we saw in this section, a model of reduction that accounts particularly well for these kinds of novelty is *limiting reduction*, which is not only compatible with the existence of novel terms in the macroscopic description, but also with a phenomenological investigation of the system that can serve as a guide to take the correct limits in the correct order. Cases of limiting reduction can be complemented with Nagelian reduction, which is based on derivability and the use of bridge laws (see Section 5.5).

A question that may arise, when we no longer understand reduction in terms of strict derivability and allow for the existence of novel terms appearing in the reduced theory and for a phenomenological investigation of the system is: What is the point of having such liberal reductions in physics? The answer to this question is that intertheoretic reduction, broadly understood as a family of models, suffices to fulfill certain goals that have motivated reductive projects in physics. I will now explain some of these goals.[43]

(i) First of all, intertheoretic reductions aim to *justify* the success of the reduced theory, by showing that the reduced theory gives a description of the phenomena that, from the perspective of the reducing theory, is *approximately correct* (e.g. in a certain limit). This goal is particularly important in cases of *diachronic reduction*, in which the reducing theory historically "replaces" the reduced theory (Nickles 1973, Fletcher, 2019). For instance, the reduction of

---

[43] See Crowther (2020) and Rosaler (2019) for an interesting discussion on the different roles of intertheoretic reductions.

Newtonian gravitation to special relativity in the limit $v/c \to 0$ may be understood as giving a justification for why Newtonian gravitation was so successful in the past. At the same time, this reductive relation may be used to justify the further use of Newtonian theory as a convenient tool for making predictions in cases in which the velocity of the body is small compared to the speed of light.

(ii) Second, in successful intertheoretic reductions, the reduced theory can be used as a *heuristic guide* for the development of the new theory (Crowther, 2020; Dizadji-Bahmani et al., 2010). For instance, the attempt of reducing the Second Law to the kinetic theory can be seen as playing a heuristic role in the development of statistical mechanics. In fact, it was the attempt of reducing the Second Law, which led Boltzmann to consider molecular distribution functions rather than the complete set of variables and to establish a close connection between entropy and probability.[44]

This heuristic goal associated with reductive enterprises in physics is especially important at the stage of theory construction, that is, when the reducing theory does not exist yet. An example of this can be found in ongoing physics, for instance, in the development of quantum gravity, which is an underdeveloped theory that describes domains in which the effects of general relativity and quantum field theory are assumed to be significant. Crowther (2020) shows how the attempt of reducing general relativity (GR) to quantum gravity (QG) works as a constraint on the latter, which means that such a reduction is paying a heuristic role in the construction of QG.

(iii) Third, the reduction of a theory to another can lead to the *explanation* of a phenomenon that cannot be explained solely on the basis of the reduced theory. A paradigmatic example of this is the explanation of the universality of critical phenomena by means of RG methods. Another example is the attempt of explaining the approach to equilibrium by reducing the so-called minus-first Law of thermodynamics to statistical mechanics (Brown and Uffink, 2001; Uffink, 2001; Valente, 2020).

(iv) Finally, intertheoretic reductions can be used to establish an *ontological dependence* of the phenomena well described by the reduced theory upon the microscopic components present in the reducing theory. This goal is not always attached to reductionistic projects, but is particularly important in cases of *synchronic reduction*, which are cases in which the two theories aim to account for the same phenomenon, but at different levels of description (usually higher levels and lower levels of description). As we saw in Section 4, the

---

[44] See Blackmore (1995) and Brush (2006) for a historical analysis on the heuristic role played by the attempt of reducing the Second Law in the development of statistical mechanics.

use of coarse-graining transformations in the reduction of a theory to another secures at least a minimal ontological dependency of the high-level theory (low-energy theory) upon the low-level theory (high-energy theory), which can be interpreted in terms of supervenience of the high-level theory upon the low level theory. In fact, for Bain (2016) this ontological dependency secures what we have called here "microphysicalism."

It is important to emphasize that the achievement of all these goals does not require the reduced theory to be strictly derived from the reducing theory without empirical input. Instead they can be achieved by a notion of reduction, which allows for approximation techniques and external guidance, and that is perfectly compatible with the notions of emergence discussed along this Element.

6 Conclusion

Throughout this Element, we explored the topic of emergence and reduction on the basis of real case studies from physics. One of our main theses was that emergence, in particular "few-many" and "coarse-grained" emergence, is compatible with reduction. This compatibilist view has been systematically defended by Butterfield in a series of papers (2011a, 2011b, 2014), but can be traced back to Anderson's seminal paper "More Is Different," in which he implicitly put forward an emergentist view of physics, while defending a reductionist picture of the word. Indeed, in the opening lines of the paper, he says:

> The reductionist hypothesis may still be a topic for controversy among philosophers, but among the great majority of active scientists I think it is accepted without question. The working of our mind and bodies, and of all the animate or inanimate matter of which we have any detailed knowledge, are assumed to be controlled by the same set of fundamental laws, which except under certain extreme conditions we feel we know pretty well. (Anderson, 1972, p. 393)

Later in the paper, he argues:

> The main fallacy in this kind of thinking is that the reductionist hypothesis does not by any means imply a "constructionist" one: The ability to reduce everything to simple fundamental laws does not imply the ability to start from those laws and reconstruct the universe. (Anderson, 1972, p. 393)

The notion of "reductionism" endorsed by Anderson corresponds to the thesis of "microphysicalism" explained in Section 1.1. This means that the notion of emergence that is implicitly defended by Anderson is *weak*, in the sense that it does not challenge microphysicalism.

In this Element, we took a step forward in this compatibilist direction, by arguing that weak emergence is not only compatible with microphysicalism, but also with intertheoretic reduction, where the latter is interpreted as a family of models (e.g. Nagelian model, limiting reduction) that can be combined in order to achieve certain epistemic and ontological goals. The achievement of these goals is by no means restricted to the possibility of deriving higher-level theories from lower-level theories without empirical input and it is perfectly compatible with the use of approximations and with a phenomenological investigation of the system. Moreover, we stressed that the use of limits and the construction of bridge laws usually requires external guidance and that, in general, the derivation of a theory from another cannot be achieved without it.

This compatibility of (weak) emergence and (intertheoretic) reduction gives rise to a new perspective on emergence, in which emergence is no longer understood as a failure of reduction, but rather in terms of positive features such as novelty and autonomy. In this sense, a behavior can be said to be *emergent* with respect to its corresponding basis, even if the theory that describes this behavior is completely *reducible* to the theory that describes its basis. For instance, in the case of few-many emergence, the behavior of many particles can be said to be emergent (novel) with respect to small samples of it, even if the theory that is used to describe the behavior of the large system can be recovered from the theory that is used to describe the behavior of small systems, by taking a certain limit or by using other approximation techniques. Analogously, a coarse-grained description can be emergent (novel and autonomous) with respect to a fine-grained description, even if the coarse-grained description can be derived from the fine-grained theory with the help of external guidance and by using mathematical limits.

Apart from defending a compatibilist view of emergence and reduction, I have also defended a pluralistic view on both emergence and reduction, in which emergence and reduction are understood as a varied landscape that serves to describe real phenomena in physics. In this Element, we focused mainly on the concepts of emergence and reduction that were more pertinent for the case-studies under investigation. Although I believe that these notions can serve to describe a wide variety of case studies that go far beyond the ones considered here, they do not necessarily cover all cases of reduction and emergence in physics. For instance, it is not clear whether the concepts developed throughout this Element can serve to describe the controversial relationship between quantum and classical mechanics, or the emergence of the Higgs Boson, even less the now disputed emergence of spacetime. The extent to which these phenomena are instances of emergence or reduction requires a detailed analysis that some philosophers and physicists have been carrying out in the past years, but such an analysis goes beyond the scope of this Element. A general conclusion to draw from this is that the specific concepts of emergence and reduction go on a pair with the scientific research. In fact, the more one delves into new case-studies from physics, the more likely it is that new concepts of emergence and reduction appear. In this sense, one should think of the concepts of emergence and reduction as dynamical concepts that are highly sensitive to the scientific research. I believe that it is this interplay between physics and philosophy that makes the topics of emergence and reduction particularly appealing and worthy of investigation in both disciplines.

References

Anderson, P. W. (1972). More is different. *Science, 177* (4047), 393–396.

Aoki, S., Boyd, G., Burkhalter, R. et al. (2000). Quenched light hadron spectrum. *Physical Review Letters, 84* (2), 238.

Ardourel, V. (2018). The infinite limit as an eliminable approximation for phase transitions. *Studies in History and Philosophy of Science Part B: Studies in History and Philosophy of Modern Physics, 62*, 71–84.

Asakawa, M., Nakahara, Y., & Hatsuda, T. (2001). Maximum entropy analysis of the spectral functions in lattice QCD. *Progress in Particle and Nuclear Physics, 46* (2), 459–508.

Bain, J. (2013a). Effective field theories. In R. Batterman (Ed.), *The Oxford handbook of philosophy of physics* (pp. 224–254). Oxford University Press.

Bain, J. (2013b). Emergence in effective field theories. *European Journal for Philosophy of Science, 3* (3), 257–273.

Bain, J. (2016). Emergence and mechanism in the fractional quantum hall effect. *Studies in History and Philosophy of Science Part B: Studies in History and Philosophy of Modern Physics, 56*, 27–38.

Bangu, S. (2009). Understanding thermodynamic singularities: Phase transitions, data, and phenomena. *Philosophy of Science, 76* (4), 488–505.

Bangu, S. (2015). Why does water boil? Fictions in scientific explanation. In U. Mäki, I. Votsis, S. Ruphy, & G. Schurz (Eds.), *Recent developments in the philosophy of science: EPSA 13 Helsinki* (pp. 319–330). Springer.

Batterman, R. W. (1995). Theories between theories: Asymptotic limiting intertheoretic relations. *Synthese, 103* (2), 171–201.

Batterman, R. W. (2001). *The devil in the details: Asymptotic reasoning in explanation, reduction, and emergence.* Oxford University Press.

Batterman, R. W. (2005). Critical phenomena and breaking drops: Infinite idealizations in physics. *Studies in History and Philosophy of Science Part B: Studies in History and Philosophy of Modern Physics, 36* (2), 225–244.

Batterman, R. W. (2011). Emergence, singularities, and symmetry breaking. *Foundations of Physics, 41* (6), 1031–1050.

Batterman, R. W. (2017). Philosophical implications of Kadanoff's work on the renormalization group. *Journal of Statistical Physics, 167* (3–4), 559–574.

Batterman, R. W. (2019). Universality and RG explanations. *Perspectives on Science, 27* (1), 26–47.

Batterman, R. W., & Rice, C. C. (2014). Minimal model explanations. *Philosophy of Science, 81* (3), 349–376.

Bayha, L., Holten, M., Klemt, R. et al. (2020). Observing the emergence of a quantum phase transition shell by shell. *Nature, 587* (7835), 583–587.

Bedau, M. (2002). Downward causation and the autonomy of weak emergence. *Principia: An International Journal of Epistemology, 6* (1), 5–50.

Berry, M. V. (2002). *Singular limits. Physics Today, 55* (5), 10–11.

Blackmore, J. T. (1995). *Ludwig Boltzmann: His later life and philosophy, 1900–1906: Book two: The philosopher* (Vol. 174). Springer Science & Business Media.

Borrmann, P., Mülken, O., & Harting, J. (2000). Classification of phase transitions in small systems. *Physical Review Letters, 84* (16), 3511.

Broad, C. D. (1925 [2014]). *The mind and its place in nature.* Routledge.

Brown, H. R., & Uffink, J. (2001). The origins of time-asymmetry in thermodynamics: The minus first law. *Studies in History and Philosophy of Science Part B: Studies in History and Philosophy of Modern Physics, 32* (4), 525–538.

Brush, S. G. (2006). Ludwig Boltzmann and the foundations of natural science. In I. M. Fasol-Boltzmann & G. L. Fasol (Eds.), *Ludwig Boltzmann (1844–1906)* (pp. 65–80). Springer.

Butterfield, J. (2011a). Emergence, reduction and supervenience: A varied landscape. *Foundations of Physics, 41* (6), 920–959.

Butterfield, J. (2011b). Less is different: Emergence and reduction reconciled. *Foundations of Physics, 41* (6), 1065–1135.

Butterfield, J. (2014). Reduction, emergence, and renormalization. *The Journal of Philosophy, 111* (1), 5–49.

Callender, C. (1999). Reducing thermodynamics to statistical mechanics: The case of entropy. *The Journal of Philosophy, 96* (7), 348–373.

Cao, T. Y., & Schweber, S. S. (1993). The conceptual foundations and the philosophical aspects of renormalization theory. *Synthese, 97* (1), 33–108.

Casetti, L., Pettini, M., & Cohen, E. (2003). Phase transitions and topology changes in configuration space. *Journal of Statistical Physics, 111* (5), 1091–1123.

Castellani, E. (2002). Reductionism, emergence, and effective field theories. *Studies in History and Philosophy of Science Part B: Studies in History and Philosophy of Modern Physics, 33* (2), 251–267.

Chalmers, D. J. (2006). Strong and weak emergence. In P. Davies & P. Clayton (Eds.) *The re-emergence of emergence*: The Emergentist Hypothesis From Science to Religion (pp. 244–256) Oxford University Press.

Crowther, K. (2015). Decoupling emergence and reduction in physics. *European Journal for Philosophy of Science, 5* (3), 419–445.

Crowther, K. (2020). What is the point of reduction in science? *Erkenntnis, 85,* 1437–1460.

Curie, P. (1895). *Propriétés magnétiques des corps a diverses températures.* Gauthier-Villars et fils.

Dizadji-Bahmani, F., Frigg, R., & Hartmann, S. (2010). Who's afraid of Nagelian reduction? *Erkenntnis, 73* (3), 393–412.

Ellis, G. F. (2020). Emergence in solid state physics and biology. *Foundations of Physics, 50* (10), 1098–1139.

Fisher, M. E. (1974). Critical point phenomena–the role of series expansions. *The Rocky Mountain Journal of Mathematics, 4*(2), 181–202.

Fisher, M. E. (1998). Renormalization group theory: Its basis and formulation in statistical physics. *Reviews of Modern Physics, 70* (2), 653.

Fisher, M. E., & Berker, A. N. (1982). Scaling for first-order phase transitions in thermodynamic and finite systems. *Physical Review B, 26* (5), 2507.

Fletcher, S. C. (2019). On the reduction of general relativity to newtonian gravitation. *Studies in History and Philosophy of Science Part B: Studies in History and Philosophy of Modern Physics, 68,* 1–15.

Franklin, A. (2018). On the renormalization group explanation of universality. *Philosophy of Science, 85* (2), 225–248.

Franklin, A. (2019). Universality reduced. *Philosophy of Science, 86* (5), 1295–1306.

Fraser, J. D. (2016). Spontaneous symmetry breaking in finite systems. *Philosophy of Science, 83* (4), 585–605.

Fraser, J. D. (2020). Towards a realist view of quantum field theory. In S. French & J. Saatsi (Eds.) *Scientific realism and the quantum* (p. 276) Oxford University Press.

Georgi, H. (1991). On-shell effective field theory. *Nuclear Physics B, 361* (2), 339–350.

Georgi, H. (1993). Effective field theory. *Annual Review of Nuclear and Particle Science, 43* (1), 209–252.

Gillett, C. (2016). *Reduction and emergence in science and philosophy.* Cambridge University Press.

Goldenfeld, N. (1992). *Lectures on phase transitions and the renormalization group.* CRC Press.

Goldstein, J. (1999). Emergence as a construct: History and issues. *Emergence, 1* (1), 49–72.

Gross, D. H. (2001). Microcanonical thermodynamics: *Phase transitions in "small" systems.* World Scientific.

Gross, D. H., & Votyakov, E. (2000). Phase transitions in "small" systems. *The European Physical Journal B-Condensed Matter and Complex Systems, 15* (1), 115–126.

Gryb, S., Palacios, P., & Thébault, K. P. (2020). On the universality of hawking radiation. *The British Journal for the Philosophy of Science, 72*(3), 809–837

Guay, A., & Sartenaer, O. (2016). A new look at emergence. or when after is different. *European Journal for Philosophy of Science, 6* (2), 297–322.

Hartmann, S. (2001). Effective field theories, reductionism and scientific explanation. *Studies in History and Philosophy of Science Part B: Studies in History and Philosophy of Modern Physics, 32* (2), 267–304.

Hendry, R. F. (2010). Emergence vs. reduction in chemistry. In C. Macdonald & G. Macdonald (Eds.) *Emergence in mind* (pp. 205–221). Oxford University Press.

Huggett, N., & Weingard, R. (1995). The renormalisation group and effective field theories. *Synthese, 102* (1), 171–194.

Humphreys, P. (2008). Synchronic and diachronic emergence. *Minds and Machines, 18* (4), 431–442.

Humphreys, P. (2016). *Emergence: A philosophical account.* Oxford University Press.

Kadanoff, L. P. (1966). Scaling laws for Ising models near T_c. *Physics Physique Fizika, 2* (6), 263.

Kadanoff, L. P. (2009). More is the same; phase transitions and mean field theories. *Journal of Statistical Physics, 137* (5), 777–797.

Kadanoff, L. P. (2010). Theories of matter: Infinities and renormalization. *arXiv preprint arXiv:1002.2985.*

Kadanoff, L. P. (2013). Relating theories via renormalization. *Studies in History and Philosophy of Science Part B: Studies in History and Philosophy of Modern Physics, 44* (1), 22–39.

Kadanoff, L. P., Houghton, A., & Yalabik, M. C. (1976). Variational approximations for renormalization group transformations. *Journal of Statistical Physics, 14* (2), 171–203.

Kim, J. (1999). Making sense of emergence. *Philosophical Studies: An International Journal for Philosophy in the Analytic Tradition, 95* (1/2), 3–36.

Knox, E. (2016). Abstraction and its limits: Finding space for novel explanation. *Noûs, 50* (1), 41–60.

Landsman, N. P. (2013). Spontaneous symmetry breaking in quantum systems: Emergence or reduction? *Studies in History and Philosophy of Science Part B: Studies in History and Philosophy of Modern Physics, 44* (4), 379–394.

Lavis, D. A., Kühn, R., & Frigg, R. (2021). Becoming large, becoming infinite: The anatomy of thermal physics and phase transitions in finite systems. *Foundations of Physics, 51* (5), 1–69.

Lorcé, C. (2018). On the hadron mass decomposition. *The European Physical Journal C, 78* (2), 1–11.

Luu, T., & Meißner, U.-G. (2019). On the topic of emergence from an effective field theory perspective. *arXiv preprint arXiv:1910.13770.*

Mainwood, P. (2006). Is more different? Emergent properties in physics. PhD thesis, Oxford University. http://philsci-archive.pitt.edu/8339

Manohar, A. V., & Wise, M. B. (2007). *Heavy quark physics.* Cambridge University Press.

Mayr, E. (1988). The limits of reductionism. *Nature, 331* (6156), 475–475.

McComb, W. D. (2004). *Renormalization methods: A guide for beginners.* Oxford University Press.

McGivern, P. (2007). Comments on Andrew Wayne's singular limits, explanation and emergence in physics. *Pacific APA meeting.*

Menon, T., & Callender, C. (2011). Turn and face the strange. . . ch-ch-changes: Philosophical Questions Raised by Phase Transitions. In R. W. Batterman (Ed.), *The Oxford handbook of philosophy of physics.* (pp. 189–223) Oxford University Press.

Mill, J. S. (1872). *A system of logic ratiocinative and inductive: 1* (Vol. 2). Longmans.

Morrison, M. (2012). Emergent physics and micro-ontology. *Philosophy of Science, 79* (1), 141–166.

Nagel, E. (1949). The meaning of reduction in the natural sciences. In R. C. Stauffer (Ed.), *Science and civilization.* (pp. 99–135) University of Wisconsin Press.

Nagel, E. (1961). *The structure of science: Problems in the logic of explanation.* Harcourt, Brace & World, Inc.

Nagel, E. (1970). Issues in the logic of reductive explanations. In H. Kiefer & K. Munitz (Eds.), *Mind, science and history* (pp. 117–137). SUNY Press.

Nickles, T. (1973). Two concepts of intertheoretic reduction. *The Journal of Philosophy, 70* (7), 181–201.

Nienhuis, B., Riedel, E., & Schick, M. (1980). Variational renormalisation-group approach to the q-state potts model in two dimensions. *Journal of Physics A: Mathematical and General, 13* (2), L31.

Nishimori, H., & Ortiz, G. (2010). *Elements of phase transitions and critical phenomena.* Oxford University Press.

Norton, J. D. (2012). Approximation and idealization: Why the difference matters. *Philosophy of Science, 79* (2), 207–232.

Norton, J. D. (2014). Infinite idealizations. In *European philosophy of science. Philosophy of science in Europe and the viennese heritage: vienna Circle Institute yearbook* (Vol. 17, pp. 197–210). Springer.

Novikov, V., Shifman, M. A., Vainshtein, A., & Zakharov, V. I. (1983). Exact gell-mannlow function of supersymmetric yang-mills theories from instanton calculus. *Nuclear Physics B, 229* (2), 381–393.

O'Connor, T., & Wong, H. (2015). Emergent properties (Stanford encyclopedia of philosophy). https://plato.stanford.edu/entries/properties-emergent/.

Palacios, P. (2018). Had we but world enough, and time... but we don't!: Justifying the thermodynamic and infinite-time limits in statistical mechanics. *Foundations of Physics, 48* (5), 526–541.

Palacios, P. (2019). Phase transitions: A challenge for intertheoretic reduction? *Philosophy of Science, 86* (4), 612–640.

Palacios, P., & Valente, G. (2021). The paradox of infinite limits: A realist response. In T. D. Lyons & P. Vickers (Eds.), *Contemporary scientific realism: The challenge from the history of science* (pp. 311–347). Oxford University Press.

Reutlinger, A. (2014). Why is there universal macrobehavior? Renormalization group explanation as noncausal explanation. *Philosophy of Science, 81* (5), 1157–1170.

Rivat, S., & Grinbaum, A. (2020). Philosophical foundations of effective field theories. *The European Physical Journal A, 56* (3), 1–10.

Robertson, K. (2020). In search of the holy grail: How to reduce the Second Law of Thermodynamics. *The British Journal for the Philosophy of Science.*

Rosaler, J. (2019). Reduction as an a posteriori relation. *The British Journal for the Philosophy of Science, 70* (1), 269–299.

Rueger, A. (2000). Robust supervenience and emergence. *Philosophy of Science, 67* (3), 466–489.

Rueger, A. (2004). Reduction, autonomy, and causal exclusion among physical properties. *Synthese, 139* (1), 1–21.

Schaffner, K. F. (1967). Approaches to reduction. *Philosophy of Science, 34* (2), 137–147.

Schmelzer, J., & Ulbricht, H. (1987). Thermodynamics of finite systems and the kinetics of first-order phase transitions. *Journal of Colloid and Interface Science, 117* (2), 325–338.

Schmelzer, J. W., Boltachev, G. S., & Abyzov, A. S. (2013). Temperature of critical clusters in nucleation theory: Generalized Gibbs' approach. *The Journal of Chemical Physics, 139* (3), 034702.

Shech, E. (2015). Two approaches to fractional statistics in the quantum hall effect: Idealizations and the curious case of the anyon. *Foundations of Physics, 45* (9), 1063–1100.

Sklar, L. (1967). Types of inter-theoretic reduction. *The British Journal for the Philosophy of Science, 18* (2), 109–124.

Sklar, L. (1999). The reduction (?) of thermodynamics to statistical mechanics. *Philosophical Studies: An International Journal for Philosophy in the Analytic Tradition, 95* (1/2), 187–202.

Smart, J. J. (1981). Physicalism and emergence. *Neuroscience, 6* (2), 109–113.

Sullivan, E. (2019). Universality caused: The case of renormalization group explanation. *European Journal for Philosophy of Science, 9* (3), 1–21.

Uffink, J. (2001). Bluff your way in the second law of thermodynamics. *Studies in History and Philosophy of Science Part B: Studies in History and Philosophy of Modern Physics, 32* (3), 305–394.

Valente, G. (2020). Taking up statistical thermodynamics: Equilibrium fluctuations and irreversibility. *Studies in History and Philosophy of Science Part A, 85*, 176–184.

Wallace, D. (2018). Spontaneous symmetry breaking in finite quantum systems: A decoherenthistories approach. *arXiv preprint arXiv:1808.09547.*

Wayne, A. (2012). Emergence and singular limits. *Synthese, 184* (3), 341–356.

Weisberg, M. (2007). Three kinds of idealization. *The Journal of Philosophy, 104* (12), 639–659.

Weiss, P. (1907). L'hypothèse du champ moléculaire et la propriété ferromagnétique. *Journal of Physics: Theories and Applications, 6* (1), 661–690.

Williams, P. (2019). Scientific realism made effective. *The British Journal for the Philosophy of Science, 70* (1), 209–237.

Wilson, K. G., & Kogut, J. (1974). The renormalization group and the expansion. *Physics Reports, 12* (2), 75–199.

Worrall, J. (1989). Structural realism: The best of both worlds? *Dialectica, 43* (1–2), 99–124.

Wu, J. (2021). Explaining universality: Infinite limit systems in the renormalization group method. *Synthese, 199*, 14897–14930.

Acknowledgments

During the past years, I have had the opportunity to discuss the ideas of this Element with outstanding physicists and philosophers of science. I am deeply grateful to Sorin Bangu, Federico Benitez, Jeremy Butterfield, Caslav Brukner, Lapo Casetti, Erik Curiel, Neil Dewar, Ben Feintzeig, Sam Fletcher, Roman Frigg, Alex Franklin, Sean Gryb, Stephan Hartmann, Laurenz Hudetz, David Lavis, Sebastian Rivat, Katie Robertson, Elay Shech, Karim Thébault, Jos Uffink, Charlotte Werndl, and Jingyi Wu.

I am also grateful to the audiences of numerous conferences and workshops, where I have presented the contents of this Element, as well as to the students of the Summer School on Mathematical Philosophy for Female Students at the Munich Center for Mathematical Philosophy (MCMP) and the students of the University of Salzburg.

I am indebted to Jim Weatherall for inviting me to write an Element on such an interesting topic and for his valuable comments on earlier versions of this Element. I also thank two anonymous referees for their helpful feedback.

My deepest gratitude goes to Giovanni Valente, who spent considerable amount of time helping me organize my thoughts and supported me in all possible ways during the production of this Element. I am also deeply grateful to Marianela P., Patricia S. and Natalia S. for giving me invaluable support during the writing process of this work.

This Element is dedicated to my daughter, Elena Sofia, who accompanied me and inspired me in her own way during the production of this work.

The Philosophy of Physics

James Owen Weatherall

University of California, Irvine

James Owen Weatherall is Professor of Logic and Philosophy of Science at the University of California, Irvine. He is the author, with Cailin O'Connor, of *The Misinformation Age: How False Beliefs Spread* (Yale, 2019), which was selected as a *New York Times* Editors' Choice and Recommended Reading by *Scientific American*. His previous books were *Void: The Strange Physics of Nothing* (Yale, 2016) and the *New York Times* bestseller *The Physics of Wall Street: A Brief History of Predicting the Unpredictable* (Houghton Mifflin Harcourt, 2013). He has published approximately fifty peer-reviewed research articles in journals in leading physics and philosophy of science journals and has delivered over 100 invited academic talks and public lectures.

About the Series

This Cambridge Elements series provides concise and structured introductions to all the central topics in the philosophy of physics. The Elements in the series are written by distinguished senior scholars and bright junior scholars with relevant expertise, producing balanced, comprehensive coverage of multiple perspectives in the philosophy of physics.

Cambridge Elements $\equiv$

The Philosophy of Physics

Printed in the United States
by Baker & Taylor Publisher Services